# BORN COUNTRY

# BORN COUNTRY

## HOW FAITH, FAMILY, AND MUSIC
## BROUGHT ME HOME

### RANDY OWEN

*with* ALLEN RUCKER

HarperOne
*An Imprint of* HarperCollins*Publishers*

HarperOne

BORN COUNTRY: *How Faith, Family, and Music Brought Me Home.* Copyright © 2008 by Randy Owen. All rights reserved. Printed in the United States of America. No part of this book may be used or reproduced in any manner whatsoever without written permission except in the case of brief quotations embodied in critical articles and reviews. For information address HarperCollins Publishers, 10 East 53rd Street, New York, NY 10022.

HarperCollins books may be purchased for educational, business, or sales promotional use. For information please write: Special Markets Department, HarperCollins Publishers, 10 East 53rd Street, New York, NY 10022.

HarperCollins Web site: http://www.harpercollins.com
HarperCollins®, ⏚ ®, and HarperOne™ are trademarks of HarperCollins Publishers

FIRST EDITION

Library of Congress Cataloging-in-Publication Data is available upon request.
ISBN 978–0–06–167314–6

08 09 10 11 12 RRD (H) 10 9 8 7 6 5 4 3 2 1

For all the kids on both sides of the families,
Owen and Teague; for all the kids round Ole Baugh Road,
Adamsburg Road, Dekalb County, the state of Alabama, and the USA
who through no fault of their own were born poor
with seemingly no way out except hard work.


And for the land I live on. Out here in the country,
there's a sense of calmness, genuineness, quietness, and
a feeling of reality of belonging and heritage that's unmatched anywhere
except in my early morning swing and the early morning shadows
on this mountain.

# CONTENTS

# BORN COUNTRY

# THE MORNING DRIVE

*Swim across the river, just to prove that I'm a man*
*Spend the day bein' lazy, just bein' nature's friend*
*Climb a long tall hick'ry. bend it over, skinnin' cats*
*Playin' baseball with chert rocks, usin' sawmill slabs for bats*

"MOUNTAIN MUSIC" BY RANDY OWEN

Relaxing is sometimes hard for me. My favorite way to relax
when I'm not making music or running my cattle operation is
to get up early in the morning and take a long, leisurely drive
around Lookout Mountain in Northeast Alabama, the place I've
lived pretty much my whole life. I have an old 1968 Ford pickup
I bought from my dad almost thirty years ago. The truck sits out
by a large gray barn under the big sign that reads: Tennessee River
Music, Inc. "Tennessee River" was the first No. 1 Alabama hit and
the first I personally wrote. It's nice to be reminded of that every
trip to the barn.

In the summer our two dogs—Hamlet, a golden retriever, and Prissy, a little Shih Tzu that belongs to our daughter Randa—will hop in the back of the truck, and the three of us will take our morning drive. In the cold weather, Hamlet and Prissy will ride up-front in the seat beside me. I drive them around like they're canine royalty. Every morning they're waiting for me by the door. They can't wait to go.

Our place on Lookout Mountain is six miles outside of Fort Payne, Alabama, in the far northeast corner of the state. Fort Payne is a small town of about thirteen thousand, known in the region as the location of a number of sock factories, or mills. Lookout Mountain is a 93-mile-long range that stretches along the northwest corner of Georgia, the northeast corner of Alabama, and the southern border of Tennessee near Chattanooga. The Tennessee part of Lookout Mountain was the scene of a number of key battles in the Civil War, including what is known as the Third Battle of Chattanooga in 1863, a decisive Union victory in which General Ulysses S. Grant decimated the last fighting force of Tennessee Rebs. There were no big battles in our area that I know of. There probably weren't enough people here to stage a fight.

Our corner of the Lookout Mountain range sits in a little nook in DeKalb County, Alabama. We're about twelve miles from the Georgia state line, ninety miles from Atlanta, and thirty-five from the Tennessee state line. We're kind of hidden away up here in the hills, a rural oasis pretty much off the beaten path of the urban South.

Our family home is right on top of the mountain, surrounded mostly by farm land, grazing land, and a lot of uncultivated timberland. After the dogs and I climb into the truck, I drive down a road just outside our property, called Baugh Road. My grandmother Owen, raised around here, was a Baugh, and many years after her death, and many years after I walked this road as a kid, I wrote the Alabama song "Ole Baugh Road." It wasn't the first song I wrote about growing up around here, or the last. And I'm still driving down the same road.

We drive to the little Wesleyan church up on the corner. I don't know the exact age of the church, but I do know that my grandfather donated some of the timber for the original structure. Though it has gone through a renovation or two, some of which I helped make, it is pretty much the same church where my mother, Martha Teague, first met my daddy, Gladstone Yeuell Owen, about sixty years ago at what is known as a Christian "singing school." On the way up to that church, we go by a little brown two-bedroom frame house that has been sitting there since my daddy moved it from its original location sometime in the 1970s. First my sister Reba lived there; then my wife, Kelly, and I moved in after we got married. Our daughter Alison had just come along, and we really needed a place to live, even a place with only a wood stove for heat. We paid my dad $3,500 for it. When Alabama hit it big, we were still living in that house. It was our first "mansion."

On the days the dogs and I turn left at the church, we follow the two-lane road past an old schoolhouse and a little store until we spot another little red brick church on the left. Behind that church is a cemetery where my daddy and my grandparents are buried, alongside a whole slew of aunts, uncles, and cousins. Probably 90 percent of my relatives who lived in this area are buried there.

We proceed to make a long, languid loop around the whole area, checking out some of the six hundred head of mostly Hereford and Angus registered cattle we have grazing on pastureland. Some of this property, formerly owned by other people we knew well, was land that my daddy sharecropped when I was growing up. My parents had their own land to tend, but they also worked other people's land to make a little extra. As the only male of three children, I was expected to work out in the fields right alongside my daddy. Cotton and corn were the main cash crops in those days. Chopping cotton in the summer and picking it in the fall is just as tedious and exhausting as you would imagine it to be. Your fingers got eaten away, but your arms got big and your back got strong.

Today, driving past those old fields, I'm drawn back to an exchange I once had with my daddy. We were out in the hot sun, picking cotton, and a plane flew over. He stopped, looked up, and said, "I wonder what it would be like to fly in a plane like that? I'd like to try that someday." Within a year or two of his passing, I could afford to fly him anywhere he wanted. And not long after that, I could have flown him around on Alabama's own plane. But it wasn't to be. He died just before Alabama took off.

We finally connect with Highway 255 and take it south down to the most beautiful site in our area of the country, the Little River Canyon. Forged by the Little River, a tributary of the bigger Coosa River, this is a surprisingly deep gorge carved into the back side of the mountain. Except for a few kayakers who come paddling down the river in the spring, few people outside of the immediate vicinity even know it's there. It's a natural wonder yet to be blemished by large parking lots and souvenir stands. Driving down to it early in the morning, we rarely meet another car on the road.

The Little River separates two counties—DeKalb County and Cherokee County. My dad was born and raised in DeKalb, and my mother was born and raised in Cherokee. For some reason the boys in DeKalb would always go looking for girls in Cherokee and never the other way around. I don't know why, but I'm glad my dad was bold enough to go a whole county away to find the love of his life.

Somewhere along the way, someone had the foresight to pave the long road that follows the rim of the canyon on the west side, not far from where some of my property ends. A few years back they repaved this rim highway, and it is now the best way to view the canyon outside of floating down the river in springtime. If you drive along that roadway, you'll maneuver numerous switchbacks over a course of twenty-six miles, not to mention take in some stunning natural scenery.

The weather on the mountain is different from that in the valley below surrounding Fort Payne. It can be three to five degrees cooler or hotter up here, depending on the time of year. And for whatever reason, we get a lot of fog. Or sometimes there's fog in the valley and it's crystal-clear up here. The atmosphere often feels more coastal than rural inland Alabama, like the way the fog rolls in and out around Carmel, California.

The canyon is absolutely beautiful most mornings. You can drive down, and there's a fog coming across the chasm, and you can't see two feet in front of your face. Then you go a hundred feet, and you're in sunshine. You look down into the gorge and see all the flowers and foliage in pristine morning light. It's pretty incredible.

At some point, usually a turnout in the road, I'll stop the truck, and the dogs will take off in search of whatever they can sniff out. I have been coming up here since I was old enough to walk—I was born in 1949. It seems so close to all I know yet so incredibly distant from how most people know me. To the millions of Alabama fans I've never met, I'm the dark-haired guy standing between two guitar-picking cousins singing about the Tennessee River or 18-wheelers or 40-hour workweeks. I usually have a shaggy beard onstage and am wearing the sweatshirt of the local high school or college football team. I'm the lead singer. Randy Owen of the group Alabama.

What the three original members of Alabama—Teddy Gentry, Jeff Cook, and I—accomplished since we first got together to play music in Jeff's living room in 1968 is hard to comprehend. For years we worked hard in clubs and bars and paid our dues, but from the day we signed with RCA Records in 1980 until our

American Farewell Tour in 2003, it felt like we were riding a bull we couldn't get off of . . . or maybe better, a runaway train. Someone asked our lifelong manager and friend, Dale Morris, to describe our rise, and he said, "From zero to a hundred overnight." That's sure what it seemed like—a country-music wildfire. Sitting on this mountain on cool summer mornings, it all seems like a distant, bygone dream until I recall all the effort, energy, and passion that went into those extremely exciting years. Every one of our forty-two No. 1 singles involved hours and hours in a recording studio, getting it right. All of those millions of albums sold signify thousands of concerts, autograph signings, and radio-station appearances. And the awards, up to and including induction into the Country Music Hall of Fame, were gifts I never expected and was humbled to receive.

In trying to describe the legacy and impact of Alabama, a lot of people turn to those dry statistics of records sold, awards won, No. 1 hits in a row, and the like, but the only people who study these statistics are insiders like record executives, PR writers, and music historians. Fans don't show up at your concerts because they consulted *Billboard* magazine and counted your hits. They're interested in the music and a good time. Period. Starting out as a bar band, living on tips and the good graces of our audiences, we knew that from the beginning. When we played "Long Train Runnin'" or "Can't See You" on a Saturday night at a nightspot called the Bowery in Myrtle Beach, South Carolina, we did it to please the crowd who had asked for it. When we played "My Home's in Alabama" before thousands of screaming fans at Nassau Coliseum on Long Island, New York, we had the same goal in mind—tear the roof off of the place and get that crowd out of their seats and jumping around and hollering for more. Alabama, record-breaking statistics aside, is in essence an audience-oriented band that forged its own definable sound and style, drew a whole new audience to country music, and made it big.

And I wouldn't have changed a minute of it.

Alabama is not through yet. The extended two-year, eighty-city farewell tour in 2003 and 2004 was an end to an often exhausting, nonstop twenty-three years of constant touring, but it wasn't a goodbye to recording and performing. We just felt it was time to slow down, see ourselves as individuals again, reintroduce ourselves to our families, and pursue some of our own pet projects. My motto these days is simple: get up in the morning and slow down. That's why it took me a couple of years to do my first solo record, which has given me immense pleasure. That's why I now alternate music with running a cattle business with my wife, Kelly. And I love working with groups like the fund-raising arm of St. Jude Children's Research Hospital, one of the true passions of my life. And that's why I'm up here on this canyon rim this morning trying to take all of this in.

Heading back home, I check out the deep foliage along the way and remember how my daddy could just reel off their varieties one by one—that's a red maple, that's a yellow maple, not to be confused with *that* tree, a post oak, or that one, a scrubby oak. He was my personal botany professor, and walking in the woods with him was both a delight and an education. He loved being outdoors. He and his friends would go foxhunting, with the goal being to chase the fox but never catch it. It was all about being in the fox's universe.

Nearing our home, I always loop back around to my mother's house, the same brick house I grew up in after my daddy, my cousin, Roland, and I built it with our own hands when I was sixteen. My mama is seventy-six and insists on living on her own, tending her own garden. The idea of moving to an assisted-living home is to her as foreign as moving to the south of France. I generally just toot the horn when I go by to let her know it's me and I'm checking on her. I usually don't stop because her dog and my dogs don't always get along, and I don't want my two jumping out and starting a fight. She looks forward to that little toot. It's my way of saying, "Good morning."

I'm a routine person, you might say, and that morning routine with the dogs is one of the great pleasures of my life. When it's time to go on the road to perform, something I've done a good part of my life since age nineteen, I don't sit around saying I can't wait to get home. But when I get here, I'm home. That's the reason, over the years since Alabama hit it big, I've acquired a lot of the land up here and tried my best to preserve and conserve it. And when I drive by the houses I've driven by and stopped by for decades, it takes me back to the people I grew up with. And I don't want to change too much of what they were about.

Or maybe I should say . . . what I'm about.

I decided to write this book, after some arm-twisting from Kelly and a few close friends, because I wanted people to know where I came from, the people who raised and nurtured me, and the outlook and values they engrained in me, hopefully values I've passed along to my own three children. As you read along, I expect you'll be reminded of some of the things I've tried to say in the music of Alabama. Of course, it's because of that music, and the millions of wonderful people who have embraced it for two and a half decades, that you even know who I am. I certainly don't speak for the group Alabama, which has always been and always will be a wholly collective effort, but in many ways the music of Alabama speaks for me.

You can only get so much into a three-minute song, no matter how many of them get played on country radio. But those songs, especially the ones I personally wrote or co-wrote, can certainly give you the *feeling* of my story. When the opening lines of "My Home's in Alabama" report that "Drinkin' was forbidden in my Christian country home" and "I learned to play the flattop on them good ol' Gospel songs," that's exactly what happened. I didn't get those lines from another country song or watching TV. I got them from my life.

So in writing this book, I guess I'll try to fill out the rest of that song and the dozens of others that were inspired by the real world I grew up in and still live in. Even today, those songs aren't very far away. Every year at Tennessee River Music, Inc., named for one song, we have our annual cattle auction—it's called Dixieland Delight, named for another song, that one written by my good buddy Ronnie Rogers. It's surprising I didn't end up naming our children "Feels So Right" and "Love in the First Degree."

This is *my* own story and *my* own version of the larger story of Alabama, the group that was *my* musical life since I was a teenager. When I say this or that happened in the history of Alabama, that's *my* impression or recollection and *mine only*. Teddy or Jeff might see it completely differently, and they might be right, or at least as right as I am. It's like when several people witness the same event like a bar fight and each tells a completely different version of what happened. If you really want to know what happened in every aspect of the Alabama story, you need to get the details from three people.

Someone once referred to me as a "cultural conservationist." I think they meant I have spent a lot of my life trying to preserve, or at least pay tribute to, the way of life I inherited from my parents and that they inherited from their kin. It's a life that is centered on a day-to-day connection with the land. You live on the land, you work it, you protect it, and you revel in its variety and beauty. You try to teach your kids the values that living on the land demands—patience, hard work, and being attuned to the rhythms of nature. In my own case, I think the family farm is an essential part of American life, and I try to do whatever I can in the state of Alabama to help young farmers-to-be get on their feet and pursue that life. As a country, we've long been dependent on foreign oil. We'll be a much different culture the day we also become dependent on foreign food.

So, living on the land is a big part of my story. So are the many, many loved ones in my life, people you don't normally read about when someone writes about the music of Alabama. I'm rooted on this mountaintop because my parents and all my aunts and uncles and cousins and assorted blood relatives are rooted here. After Kelly and I got married, I brought her here to live, and, thank God, she settled right in and learned to love it like I do. In an age where people move around so much they don't know how to answer the question "So, where are you from?" this is a story of what you can gain by never leaving where you're from. There are sacrifices, for sure—there always are—but at least in my life, I found a reality here at home that helped me survive the kind of high-stakes career in music that has damaged or destroyed some of the most talented people on earth.

Finally, the music of Alabama, and my own personal music, came from the music we heard all our lives, the rich Southern tradition of gospel music and the God for whom that music was created in order to help folks worship and celebrate. From my earliest memory, this music was part of my life. I come from a multigenerational gospel-music family. Until the two inspirational albums we recently released, Alabama rarely sang about God, but trust me, God was present at every concert. The faith of my father and mother, both expressed in the music they played and in the life they aspired to lead, runs deep in both my personal life and in the songs Alabama sang every night.

My mama, as I said, lives and thrives right down the road, and I look forward to every breakfast of homemade biscuits and "syrip 'n' butter" at her house. My daddy died suddenly in 1980, right at the start of the Alabama success story, while I was on my way to Myrtle Beach. Because of that, I suffered a wound that has never quite healed. Of all the people on earth, my daddy was the one person I wanted to succeed *for*. As his only son, I idolized him. He taught me to hunt, fish, laugh, farm, persevere, build a fire, and play the guitar. In my pursuit of music, he was my number one fan and greatest inspiration. In so many ways, he taught me how to live.

This is my story and no one else's, but in large part, it's the story of a father and a son. Daddy, this book's for you.

# CHAPTER 1

# HOME

*Round Ole Baugh Road,*
*Is a great place for kids to grow*
*Some grow up and move away*
*Most of us decide to stay*
*Round Ole Baugh Road.*
*The neighborhood still looks the same*
*just new kids with the same old names*
*My Baugh Road's in a Southern state*
*Yours may be anywhere, USA*
*Look around for your Baugh Road.*

"OLE BAUGH ROAD" BY RANDY OWEN

My daddy's name is Gladstone Yeuell Owen. My middle name is Yeuell, and so is my son, Heath's. Why his parents gave him such an unusual name, I have no idea. His brothers had more familiar names like Johnny, Albert, Virgil, Riley, and Grady. Mama and some of Daddy's close relatives always called him Gladsten, but the rest of the world just shortened it to G.Y. It made life a whole lot simpler.

I really don't know much about my daddy's side of the family beyond two or three generations back. We've always assumed that the name Owen was Welsh, but I also remember my grandfather, Joseph Ernest Owen, throwing around terms like Scotch-Irish and Black Dutch when I used to pester him as a kid about our family roots. "Black Dutch" was a term used by Anglo-Saxons that referred to anyone with dark complexion of European ancestry. It was also used by American Indians to hide their Indian ethnicity during the time they were less than second-class citizens. I know I have some Indian blood in me, but as to how much and what tribe or strain, I'm clueless.

The Owen family saga I know best begins with my grandfather Owen. Sometime after the Civil War, my grandfather's mother, whose family name was Hester, was living around Armuchee, Georgia, about thirty miles east from where I'm writing this. She had apparently lost her husband, my great-grandfather, perhaps in the war or from pneumonia—I've heard both theories—and married a guy a good fourteen or fifteen years her junior. Because of four years of the bloodiest carnage ever on American soil, good men in the South were hard to find, so she did the best she could, no doubt.

There was just one catch. Husband number two didn't want her two very young children, including my grandpa, around. So my grandpa and his sister Josie, after some period of time, were shipped off to his own grandparents in DeKalb County. They came over in a horse-drawn wagon. There they were raised by my great-great-grandparents Hester and never returned to their home in Georgia.

I got the feeling, as a kid, that my grandfather never cared for his mother and the way she had abandoned her own children. He never said anything bad about her. He just never said anything, period. My cousin Jackie and I once rode our motorcycles over to the Armuchee/Little Sand Mountain area of Georgia to look for our great-grandfather's burial site, but we could never find it. Years later, I located my great-grandmother's grave at a cemetery in the area called Walker's Chapel. It listed her as Mattie Owen, even though her second husband, named Frank Lindsey, is buried right next to her. I think my family designed her tombstone and went out of their way to keep his name off it, though they were officially man and wife. There was not a lot of love between the two families, it's pretty clear, even when it came to grave markers.

My grandparents, Joseph and his wife, Sena SeBell Baugh Owen, lived here all their lives. They had a slew of children and grandchildren. The house my daddy grew up in still stands just a few miles away. It would probably take me all day to drive around this immediate area and say hello to all my cousins, aunts, uncles, nieces, and nephews who came from this one branch of our family tree. Growing up in the 1950s and '60s, you could go to a community event like a sing-in and half the crowd would be immediate kinfolk or extended-family members. You were always among "your" people, and I loved them all. For me, every family get-together was like a trip to Disneyland.

My mother, born Martha Alice Teague, was the third of seven children of Henry Baughton Teague Sr.—my beloved "Paw Paw"—and Velma Cloe Goodman Teague. All the kids were raised up on a farm in Cherokee County, situated on the eastern ridge of Lookout Mountain where the land was hard, gravelly, and unforgiving. "Over in the valley," my daddy referred to that area. My Paw Paw raised cotton and corn and worked as a logger when he could. The milk cows got the corn, and the cottonseed and the cotton itself were sold to make ends meet. With all those mouths to feed on subsistence farming, those ends seldom met.

My mother claims to this day, "I won't take nothing for it. It made good children out of all of them," she says. The lesson was early and clear: if you got anything, you had to work for it. They were the poorest of the poor, but they never went hungry, even during the worst years of the Depression. My mother often had to walk to school without a long coat in the winter, just a hand-me-down jacket or sweater, but I never heard her complain much about it. In fact, I've never heard her complain much about anything.

I'm sure my mother's growing-up years were far from the often sentimental image of the noble, salt-of-the-earth rural farm family, but despite the obvious hardships and limitations—my mama had an eleventh-grade education—she and all her siblings survived and thrived. Of the seven children in her family, all now in their seventies and eighties, only one has passed away, and that was only a few months back. A hard life created a hardy stock, that's for sure.

The key component in her family life beyond work was faith. Both of my parents come from the Southern Holiness tradition, a set of Christian beliefs that shares some similarities with early Methodism and modern Pentecostalism but is also distinctly different in many ways. I know from my own upbringing that the Holiness faith my parents practiced placed a high premium on the idea of living a holy life, a life that was free of what they considered sinful practices. More than what particular church you attended or what denomination you identified with, the emphasis was on how you lived your personal life and how you taught your children to live theirs. It was the kind of religious practice that focused on the community, not a greater religious organization or label like Methodist, Baptist, or the like. Many of the churches my parents attended and where they performed music were nondenominational. Today, for instance, some of my family attends the Rainsville Community Church, a nondenominational congregation. My sister Reba says she likes it because all of the offerings and other donations stay right in the community and aren't divvied up with a large national association.

One expert described the Holiness ethic as "no smoking, no drinking, no cardplaying, and no theatergoing." There weren't too many theaters, at least not live theaters, in rural Alabama to lure you off the straight and narrow, and my daddy smoked at one point in his life, but I was certainly raised to abstain from drinking and to be very leery of what came across the radio and television. I don't remember the issue of cardplaying coming up. This was long before there were legal Native American bingo parlors in Alabama and floating casinos anchored off the coast of Mississippi.

My mama remembers her daddy carrying her to church as a very young child. The church didn't have Holiness in the name—it was a Wesleyan Methodist church—but in my mama's words, "they believed in people being clean and walking upright," so it passed the test. From the very first time she attended church, she remembered her daddy singing. By all accounts he was an out-standing singer. His mother's maiden name was Speer, and even people with only a passing appreciation of Southern gospel music know of the Speer Family as a legendary, multigenerational singing institution. I can't say for sure if I'm related to those Speers or not, but it's nice to imagine.

My grandmother Teague was apparently no musician, nor could she carry a tune. My grandfather, the singer, didn't have any instruments around the house because he couldn't afford them. He did play a mouth harp but had to be careful playing it at home because the dogs would start howling and wake up the neighbors. For some reason, dogs get very excited at the sound of a mouth harp.

The only instrument my granddaddy did buy was a big upright piano that is still in the family. He bought it mainly for his three oldest girls, including my mother. He wanted a piano around because he loved directing group singing and he didn't have anyone to play for him. The piano cost him $210, a king's ransom for a poor tenant farmer from Cherokee County, Alabama, in the 1940s, but I doubt he ever regretted his decision. At least one of his daughters (Mama) and Mama's brother Charles became terrific piano players and passed on a rich gospel-music tradition to a whole new generation of offspring, including me, Martha's black-haired son.

My mother and her sisters each took a total of seven piano lessons from an old man in the area named Jim Sparks. The deal was that he would charge a dollar a lesson for the two older girls and the little one would get to learn free. The little one was my mother. She walked two miles in snow every Saturday to learn to play. Her sisters lost interest quickly. After the seven lessons, my mother just kept on teaching herself. As she recalls, "I just went to work at it."

My daddy loved music, too, with a passion. He, too, came from a musical family. He loved to sing and could play a little piano and fiddle, but mainly concentrated on the guitar. Pretty early in my life, I realized he harbored a long-standing dream to be a professional musician. He had great love for some leading country musicians of his time, like Martha Carson, Little Jimmy Dickens, and the great Merle Travis, whose famous picking style, called thumb picking, he tried to emulate. His emotional release, like mine, was music. In many ways, my life is the product of that dream.

A few years before I came along, Daddy even tried his hand at recording. Sometime in the mid-1940s, he got together with his brother, Blackie, and their cousin, Sonny, and formed a trio called Stony, Blackie, and Sonny. Daddy was Stony, a shortened version of Gladstone. They went into a studio and recorded two songs on a 78, one side being "Let's Say Goodbye Like We Said Hello" and the flip side being "Just to Know You Still Remember Me." Daddy, as he always did, sang harmony and played lead guitar. I remember being all of nine years old when I heard that recording for the first time. I was very impressed.

This one early stab at musical stardom came after Gladstone Owen married Martha Teague, having met and fallen in love specifically because of their common interest in music. They first met in 1945 at the hallowed Southern institution called a "singing school," which happened, as I said, to take place at the Wesleyan Methodist church up on the corner, which we pass every time we leave the farm and head to town. My mama was fifteen years old and as a dozen old photographs make clear, she was a real looker. My dad was twenty-six going on twenty-seven and in Mama's words, "a black-headed, black-eyed handsome dude," almost six feet in height. She goes on to say he had "a lot of boy in him," which anyone who ever knew him could attest to. He was the kind of guy who was always full of foolishness and laughter and fun. My mother's family, and to a certain extent my mother, was more on the sober side. It was a match of personalities made in heaven or, at least, singing school.

"He didn't act hardly like he was that old or nothing," Mama now reports. "He'd never been married. He was just a good, clean farm boy."

A singing school is a long-standing cultural tradition in the American South. These itinerant music programs were actually created in the Northeast in the early days of Protestant America to pass along spiritual music and underscore the importance of group or congregational singing in worship services. At some point they migrated to the South and took hold. The purpose of a singing school in my parents' day was to teach hymns, new and old, to anyone in the community who wanted to learn, and especially young people. The music was usually taught using sight reading and a form of musical notation called shape note.

Shape notes were just that—notes in distinct shapes like a square or a triangle, which made it relatively easy for an amateur to follow a tune. Shape-note music has been around for two centuries in the American South and allows different groups of singing-school participants to learn different parts of a song. The bass voices would learn the bass shape notes, the altos would learn their own line of notes, and so on. The idea was for everyone in the church or musical gathering to participate in the singing in a serious way, not just mumbling the lyrics of some hymnal selection. My mama calls this "convention type" singing as opposed to a musical group or a choir in the front of the sanctuary. Sacred-harp singing, a pure a cappella style of Southern church singing where the altos stand in one section of the hall and the tenors in another, was also practiced in this area of Alabama and North Georgia, but it wasn't the tradition of my parents.

Singing schools were the way that sacred songs became popular, not to mention a major social event for rural families.

Many of the songs written by the great gospel composer Albert Brumley—classics like "I'll Fly Away" (featured in the film *O Brother, Where Art Thou?*) and "Turn Your Radio On"—were first heard at singing schools. Laura Ingalls Wilder, author of *Little House on the Prairie,* attended a singing school. So did I when I was growing up, but my own interest went far beyond learning new gospel songs. I was mainly there to meet girls.

The singing school where my parents met ran for two weeks in the summer, when the twenty-five or so participants weren't in school and weren't needed on the farm to either plant or harvest. Mr. Sparks, the old man who taught my mama to play the piano, was in charge of the school, and he asked my grandfather if his teenage daughter could come over and be the chief accompanist. (Mr. Sparks couldn't actually *play* the piano, only teach it.) My mama had an aunt named Sophronia who lived across the road from the church at the time, so her dad said fine, she could make the trek all the way from "the valley" to help out.

Mama loved playing for that singing school. It was the first time she had ever done anything like that. It gave her a spurt of confidence to master and play those new songs in front of all those people. She clearly liked to perform. Sixty-plus years later, she is still playing gospel music before church and community groups every chance she can get.

As she tells the story, on the very first morning of the school, her dad brought her over in his 1936 Ford and dropped her off at her aunt's doorstep. While she waited on the front porch for her aunt to come to the door, she looked across the street and saw tall, dark, and handsome Gladstone, her husband-to-be, sitting on the church steps waiting for school to begin. According to her, he saw this teen beauty across the way and whistled at her. "Needless to say," she now reports, "I just looked away."

After the singing school ended, they kept bumping into each other—Mama even played at G.Y.'s grandmother's funeral—and soon he started writing her letters, many of which she still has. As soon as he could get his hands on a car, he'd drive over the mountain and visit. Their main going-out date was to a convention-type, open-invitation singing event. As Mama says, it was "a clean place to go." These sing-ins usually happened on Sunday afternoons all over the area. The level of musical sophistication among these poor, largely uneducated rural farming people was high. Many would venture from one church to another on Sunday afternoons to sing in harmony with their neighbors, most of whom had learned their parts in a singing school. It was both soul nourishing and fun.

My mama, then as now, accompanied the group singing on piano. And then as now, she played shape-note music. She says she never got around to learning "round note" or conventional music notation, because she could just glance at the shapes and know exactly where the music was headed.

After about two years of courting and singing together, my parents got married in July of 1947 and settled down to a life of farming and raising kids. My Paw Paw Teague gave them two wedding presents: a crippled Jersey heifer and a fifty-pound sack of white potatoes. Daddy traded the heifer for a milk cow that turned out to have no milk. About that time, their first farming mule, Ole Kate, died of bloating after Daddy overfed her after a hard day's work. So with no mule or cow, he had to rent a mule, Ole Dixie, from his daddy to finish the crop. It cost him $25, but as with most things, he got it done.

To this day, my mama considers my daddy the finest man she ever met. She says he was "as steady as a rock." He was also a joy to be around. He played every instrument in the band and knew certain aspects of music much better than she did at the time. She learned to play strictly by ear, aided by shape notes. He taught her keys and chord progressions. As soon as they could raise enough cash to buy their own piano, they were a two-person musical team.

At every opportunity, they would head off to a church and a singing session. Often they went by foot, lugging G.Y.'s guitar and small amplifier. Mama remembers the two of them traips-ing right across a pasture I now own on their way to the corner church to play and sing with the neighbors. I can stand in that field today and feel what it must have been like to be the two of them, young and in love, headed by foot to a local songfest, my daddy no doubt popping jokes and my mama laughing and haul-ing his general-store amplifier.

Mama says it best: "We'd just play with whoever sung. We went to gatherings, everybody sung, just whoever felt like singing a song just started up. And hang on if you didn't have the rhythm."

Their life was hard, but in Mama's mind, "We had a good time, don't you know." She once told me, "One of the most enjoyable days of a man's life, if he's got a companion that loves

him, is when they're striving to accomplish something. They're
working together. And they can do about anything they set their
minds to do."

That was my parents' early life. They started out without
much, but the Lord blessed them and kept us all safe and well
fed, even in the worst of times. It was not only a hard life, it was
a strict life according to the tenets of their faith. Both my sister
Reba and I grew up without a radio or a television set. We got our
first radio when I was about twelve. My mama has a TV today, an
old console type from the 1960s, but rarely watches anything but
a Sunday-afternoon recording of the Gaither Homecoming Tour.
Of course, there was never a drop of alcohol in our house. At a
distance, this kind of strict living might seem oppressive. Growing up, it just seemed normal.

I was the first born, in 1949, followed shortly by my sister
Reba. My second sister, Rachel, didn't come along until I was thirteen and Reba was eleven. She never went to a singing school and
never knew life without radio or TV, but she certainly learned
music at the feet of Mama and Daddy and joined them in the first
grouping of the singing Owen Family. Today Kelly and I have the
same mix of kids, two daughters and one son, though in slightly
different order. I guess it's a family tradition.

When I was about four, my parents scrapped up every dime
they had and bought forty acres of land up on Lookout Mountain, then called the McMichen place. The house was an old-style
wood-frame house with a great porch swing. They focused at
first on growing cotton and corn and later grew mainly corn, hay,

and timber. My daddy always had a few cattle around. He loved livestock and the buying and selling of cattle.

We were poor, no doubt about it. I remember one year when I was old enough to add and subtract, I decided to play CPA and calculate our family's annual income. It came to a grand total of $800. A year of farming your own land; raising cattle, hogs, and chickens; sharecropping on other people's land; and selling what you could—all for a yearly gross income of $800. That was around 1960, and according to a conversion site on the Internet called MeasuringWorth.com, $800 in 1960 equals about $5,600 today. In other words, not much.

But we got by. We raised our own potatoes and vegetables, ate our own meat, and canned everything that could fit in a can. One year when the season was terribly dry and the corn didn't come up, Reba and I got together and plowed a field and raised these gigantic Congo watermelons—thirty and forty pounds each—and sold them to local country grocery stores. We figured out ways like that to earn money. We had electricity but didn't use it all that much. Our light bill, I remember, was one dollar a month. We cooked on a wood-burning stove and heated the house by a wood-burning fireplace. We had chickens who liked to crawl in the space under the house and lay eggs. It was my job, at age seven or eight, to crawl under there on my belly to retrieve them. To this day I recall the time I shimmied under there and somehow got stuck in a tight spot between the earthen floor and the floorboards of our house. I completely freaked out. I couldn't get out, and no one could hear me down there. I finally figured my way out of that trap and lived to tell about it, but it was a claustrophobic moment that still haunts me.

I know, probably to some of you raised in the suburbs, this all sounds like a sad old country song—raised poor, crawling under the house for breakfast, stoking the wood fire on a winter's day—but it wasn't sad, and those rural routines made for a rich and vigorous existence. There were tough times, for sure, times when my parents were frustrated or discouraged about their lot in life, but I have a tendency to block out those memories, to let them go and move on. This is probably a survival technique I learned early on to protect myself against bitterness and discouragement. Envy and jealousy can eat away at you, and the only person who is generally harmed is yourself. I don't really know where I got the instinct to eliminate bad memories, but it has served me well over the years.

In general, though, we weren't embarrassed to be poor—we didn't even *feel* poor most of the time. We were surrounded by uncles, aunts, and cousins who were in the same situation, and since we weren't glued to the radio or TV, we didn't envy the rich people who paraded across the screen. My sister Reba and I were only twenty-three months apart in age, so we largely entertained ourselves, with the help of all those cousins. Reba contends that I was never in a picture that she wasn't in too. I either had my arm around her or was holding her as a baby. We were inseparable and we had plenty to keep us amused. We had two imaginary friends—Pooterst and Chillynx—to keep us amused. Plus, we had real live cousins like Jackie and Donnie Owen to play with, and we had all of Northeast Alabama as our playground.

Like all kids in the country, we were very close to our pets. One of our favorite hens was Groucho, a Rhode Island Red. When she disappeared one day, Reba and I were beside ourselves with grief. Even on a grand car ride to a family reunion with our great aunt and uncle, Troy and Edith Payton, all we could do was worry about Groucho. Two weeks later we finally found her camping out in a mule-drawn seed planter. I couldn't wait to crawl under the house to get her next batch of eggs.

Dogs were our constant companions. Ole Lead, an English shepherd who had survived a rattlesnake bite in my aunt Goldie's garden, couldn't survive when the mule-drawn mowing machine accidentally mangled his right back leg. Joker, our black-and-tan beagle, took off with me and some friends to the canyon to go swimming one day and never came home. I'd spend hours with Joker on the front-porch swing, swaying his paw around like he was directing a song at one of the singing schools.

In our free time, we were allowed to roam wherever we wanted. We either walked or bummed a ride from a passing truck. It was a given that if you saw someone on the road while you were driving by, you'd stop and let the person hop on the running board and hold on to the window for a quick ride. If you didn't stop, everyone on the mountain knew about it before nightfall.

But our main activity as kids, other than school, was working alongside our folks. Besides raising livestock and much of the food we ate, my daddy farmed forty acres of his own land and then often sharecropped other land. There were two forms of sharecropping he practiced. One was straight sharecropping, where you work another person's land, split the cost of fertilizer and seed, and literally "share" the crop that is produced on some proportional basis—halves, or thirds, or fourths. The second form we called "standing rent." In this arrangement you rented the land from someone for a fixed price and then reaped the benefits of the entire crop. To pull this off, you had to have the money to pay the rent and all the farming costs going in, or you had to be able to borrow it. It was always more expensive to do a standing-rent arrangement than a straight sharecropping one. And if the crop was bad, you might really take a bath.

It was a struggle for my parents for most of my growing-up years. I remember one year, all we seemed to eat was peas and okra. I don't know what happened to the other vegetables, but it was peas and okra almost every night. If we went somewhere else to eat, they'd ask what I wanted, and I'd say peas and okra. I guess that was comfort food for me, at least that year. We always had homemade cornbread, of course, and chicken and eggs, so we got by just fine.

I didn't mind working alongside my daddy in the fields, but the burden of responsibility he constantly carried was distressing to me. I took it personally. I adored my father and hated to see him upset or anxious. Seeing the hurt and worry on his face over how much he'd have to borrow next year to make a crop or how he was going to make his tractor payment that fall or what kind of crop was coming up in the fields—I took it all in like it was *my* responsibility. The weather was always a source of anxiety—too little or too much rain could ruin an entire growing season and throw the whole family into financial distress. When my daddy stayed up nights worrying about all of this, I stayed up too. I think I was different from most farm kids in that regard. It was just my nature, I guess.

I remember one year when I was about eleven, I decided I was going to give my mama and daddy a big lift and turn all the soil before the spring planting season. Turning the soil is where you break up all the old soil and allow it to aerate before you plant a new crop. We had a little 1953 Ford Jubilee tractor, bought used from Otis Mitchell for $1,250, and I set out to turn about forty or fifty acres. This included all our family land plus some land we were working under a standing-rent deal.

The day I finished that job was probably the proudest day of my eleven-year-old life. I had really lightened my daddy's considerable load.

Mama worked just as hard as Daddy. She milked cows, fed chickens, canned vegetables, and even churned butter. She churns her own butter to this day. Her only nod to modern times is that she now churns with an electric churning machine. The butter makes itself, she says. All she's got to do is clean the machine afterward.

Plus, she made all our clothes. She could make anything. When I was going to grade school, she made everything I wore— pants, shirt, even my cap. As Reba remembers, Mama was so good that she would spot a new dress in a Sears, Roebuck catalog and proceed to make it without a pattern. Later on, Mama wrote a gospel song that included the lines, "If the garment fits you well, the pattern you must know." It was an analogy about instinctively knowing the way of the Lord, but Reba says every time she hears those lines, she remembers the seeming miracle of Mama's making a dress that fit from scratch, already knowing the pattern.

As I said, Mama was quite the looker in her day, and though we didn't have money for fancy clothes for her, she figured out a way of getting some. Her aunt Mary, my great aunt, lost her husband due to injuries from World War I when she was in her early twenties and then suffered the cruel fate of losing her son in World War II. The son, named L.C., had graduated from Auburn and soon after got his wings as a navy pilot. He went down on his first or second mission, never to be found.

Aunt Mary, as we all called her, left Cherokee County, moved to Montgomery, and got a good job at the Alabama DMV. She was a young, single, attractive woman, and the suitors apparently lined up at her door. She would occasionally bring one of her boyfriends up to see us, and they always seemed to drive Cadillacs and throw around money. They would beg Mama to get Aunt Mary to marry them. She was obviously a major catch and in no big hurry to be tied down.

In any case, these gentlemen callers also bought Aunt Mary clothes, lots of clothes, and when she tired of them, she'd box them up and send them to her sweet niece Martha. It was like Christmas every time one of those boxes arrived. They were hand-me-downs, but they were the finest hand-me-downs in the house, and Mama looked great in them. Later on, my mother took Aunt Mary in as she got older until finally the onset of Alzheimer's disease forced her to put my aunt in a nursing home.

Later on in her own life, in the early 1970s, Mama began to take what she would call a "public" job, i.e., a paying job off the farm. As I mentioned earlier, Fort Payne is renowned in the South as a sock-mill town, mostly a center of production of sports and children's socks. The landscape of the town is peppered with small- and medium-size sock factories. Reba, Rachel, and I all did our stint making socks in our younger years. Many of these sock mills have long shut down since this kind of manual labor moved either across the border or overseas as part of the global economy. But there is still an active sock-making business around here, and for twenty plus years—long after Alabama had hit it big and I could easily afford to help supplement her income—Mama punched in and made socks.

Her specialty was sewing toes, using a big industrial sewing machine. Nothing but toes. And in her words, "Believe you me, I reckon I thought I had to do more than anybody," so she often passed on the opportunity to get up from her workstation and relax in the middle of the day. If her back hadn't given out after twenty years of sewing toes, she'd probably still be working there today. Hard work, in her mind, was part of a clean life, a message I got at a very young age.

Borrowing money was also a way of life for small-farm people like my parents. That year they made all of $800, they probably had to borrow $400 and pay it back with interest. Every spring they had to make a trip to the local bank to borrow enough to plant a crop and then pray to God that they'd make enough from selling the cotton to repay the loan in the fall. My daddy was a stickler about paying this money back. His word was pretty much the only collateral he had.

Years later, when I was on the board of the same bank (now Compass Bank) where he used to borrow money, I heard a great story about my dad. One morning, G.Y., as they all called him, walked into the bank to borrow $700. He was planning to buy some cows, go through all the work of getting them on the truck and hauling them down to the stockyards, and then hopefully sell them at a profit. The banker said sure and handed him the money.

Later that very same day, the banker sees G.Y. coming back down the sidewalk. He walks in and hands the guy his $700 back, plus half a day's interest. He had driven out to the cattle farm, gotten the cattle, hauled them back to the stockyards, sold them, got immediate payment, and marched right to the bank, all in a span of a few hours.

The banker had a big laugh. "Hell, G.Y.," he said, "I can't make any money like that. You're borrowing money in the morning and paying it back in the afternoon!" My daddy got the joke but was still glad he had paid that debt so fast.

It's often the smallest of details in matters like this that make the deepest impressions. For instance, later when I was in college, I bought a 1972 yellow-and-black Camaro and borrowed the money from the Farm Bureau to pay for it, with my daddy cosigning. The payments, I remember, were $34.98 a month. One month I wrote that check with only $35 in the bank, and it still cleared. My new balance: two cents.

My daddy told me, "When you're ready to make the next-to-last payment, make two, and pay the thing off a month early." I did as he said and got a nice note back from the Farm Bureau that if I ever needed another loan, to give a call. I called them and asked if I'd need my daddy to co-sign the next loan too. They said, "No, son, your signature is good enough now." With that one small gesture, my word was now as good as my daddy's.

During my early years, Daddy mostly farmed, but later in life raising crops took a backseat to trading cattle. He loved the cattle business. For a couple of years he worked directly for his cattle sales outfit in order to learn the ins and the outs of the trade. But mostly he bought and sold commercial cows and calves. He would have loved to have had registered cattle, a business I'm in today, but he couldn't afford them. Like many things in my life, my own interest in cattle is probably an extension of his dream.

On one occasion when I was a kid—an occasion indelibly imprinted in my brain—my dad bought some cattle that had originated with a guy from Florida. Nothing seemed out of the ordinary until the day a federal inspector and the sheriff showed up at our front door. The sheriff, I remember to this day. His name was Harold Richards. They were there to arrest my dad on a charge in trafficking in stolen cattle.

My dad had no earthly idea what they were talking about, and I was scared to death that they were going to haul my daddy off to jail. But Harold Richards, who knew my dad well, wasn't buying the charge. He told the inspector, "Well, I'll tell you one thing, I'm not going to arrest G.Y. Owen." The inspector replied,

"Well, he's got stolen cattle in his possession." "Well," said the sheriff, "there's some other explanation for it."

I remember the grief this caused my dad and the sleepless nights when he thought he was going to prison for some scam he didn't even know existed.

The straightforward explanation finally came out. The guy in Florida was reporting his cattle stolen so he could collect insurance money, then shipping them to Alabama and selling them to people like my daddy. In other words, the man was getting paid twice for the same cow. Once they figured this all out, my dad was no longer in trouble, but the feeling of injustice has stayed with me forever.

This kind of screwup happened more than once. Federal officials and other experts with badges would show up at our farm on occasion and ask a lot of insinuating questions about our livestock. But it was probably that first time that did the trick for me. I have always had a real tough spot in my heart for officials like that. They invariably treated my dad like a criminal, a really good man who was as honest as they come. To this day I still resent that feeling I got then of being pushed around and looked down on.

But most of the time my daddy was a card and a cutup. We'd come in from the fields at night, and Daddy would be ready to play with us. As with a lot of families, city and country, Mama was more often the serious one, the taskmaster, and Daddy was the entertainer. I love my mother to death and feel that I am as much a product of her as I am of him, but Daddy had energy and mischief to burn.

He was a great swimmer, for instance, one of the most awesome swimmers I ever knew. It was part of that boyish enthusiasm he had for the outdoors. He loved the water and would swim up, sideways, backward, for hours. Mama couldn't swim at all. Daddy tried to teach her a hundred times, but it didn't take.

He loved to drive like a madman on the mountain's country roads—fishtailing, squealing tires, scaring his kids half to death. He loved car racing, at least as far as listening to NASCAR on the radio. We didn't have a radio for years, but when we finally got one, Daddy and I would tune in a race and listen to the crash-by-crash broadcast. His own favorite car trick was to fill our car up with gas—never more than a dollar's worth, as I remember— then shut the engine off at the top of every hill in the area so we'd pretty much coast off the mountain into town. I loved it. It was like riding a soapbox-derby car, a free ride. At the bottom of the hill, he'd pop the clutch and roar on down the road.

And he told stories. In a house with no radio and TV and a life far from town, storytelling was a major form of entertainment, and my daddy was good at it. Back in the days when foxes were plentiful around the mountain, my dad and his buddies would go on overnight fox hunts, and I'd tag along every chance I could. It was a social outing more than anything. They'd march out into the woods, wearing their Liberty overalls and accompanied by their favorite fox dogs, bring along a pint jar full of pinto beans and cornbread all mixed together, build a fire, and tell stories.

Oh, yeah, they'd finally get around to turning the fox dogs loose to hunt down a fox—to "sic 'em" or "cast 'em." You could tell by a dog's bark whether he had succeeded in treeing a fox, but it didn't really matter all that much. They never shot one, to my knowledge. They loved the foxes and never intended to kill one. It was all about the chase, and the storytelling.

One of my favorite fox stories involved a dog Daddy called Old Red. Daddy loved the dog and felt bad about selling him, but a man from Rock City, Georgia, almost forty miles from our farm, offered a hundred dollars, and Daddy couldn't turn the money down. Most people back then wouldn't pay anywhere near a hundred hard-earned dollars for a fox dog, even a good one. Daddy would tell us about one old boy who was looking for a dog with a good "squalling mouth." Someone offered to sell him one for a hundred bucks, and his reply was, "Oh, good God, no. If I had to pay a hundred dollars for a fox dog, I'd squall louder than the dog!"

One day, my dad and my uncle Virgil were sitting around, and Daddy was bemoaning the fact that he no longer had Red to "put in" on a fox. Virgil walked out to the road, turned to Daddy, and said, "Well, here he is, right here." The dog had jogged home from Rock City, and it was clear that if Daddy had taken him back to his now-rightful owner, he would have just turned around and come back to our farm. The man under-stood that the dog was never going to switch homes, so they worked out a new deal for Red to stay with us. Which made perfect sense to me. Here he had a beautiful canyon and woods and open fields to run foxes on. If I were a fox dog, I wouldn't leave here either.

As my sister Reba would certainly confirm, Daddy held center stage in our family. Next to him, I was the quiet one. I never wanted the spotlight. It was reserved for him. I was shy, undemanding, and easygoing. Certainly early on, Reba got into a lot more trouble at school than I did. If I got worked up about something, I generally held it inside and rarely showed it to the outside world. Even when I began to take an interest in music, my goal was to learn the guitar and play in the background but never to sing, let alone be the lead singer. And even when I began to sing onstage, I never wanted to *talk* or dance around onstage.

But when I finally came out of my shell and began to put myself out there, I always had one good model to point the way—my fun-loving daddy.

In general, I was the son of a farmer—or as Mama first described Daddy, "a good clean farm boy"—the first twelve years or so. People ask me all the time, "Why do still live up there?" Why do I choose, a lifetime later, to live so close to my childhood home, right down to the same acres of land I farmed with my father and so close to my mother, my sisters, and all the other relatives within shouting distance?

The answer is always the same: because this is home.

I could live somewhere else. I could live anywhere, really, as long as Kelly went along with the decision. Country performers these days live all over the world. They come to Nashville to record and attend industry functions like the CMA Awards or Fan Fair. Otherwise, they are on the road much of the year, living out of a touring bus, and then go home to places as wild and exotic as an island in the Caribbean, a house in Jamaica, a farm in Australia, or a beachfront home in Hawaii.

For whatever reason, I've never had the desire to live in any of those places. I love to visit them and visit friends who live there. Some stars have two or three homes. I've always only had one home. Here. At home.

It's pretty simple, really. If I relocated to any other spot on earth, it might be heavenly, but it wouldn't be comfortable. It wouldn't be where my heart is and near the hearts of my mother, my two sisters, all my other blood relations, and now my children. This mountain is our heart. This mountain is our home.

I think it all goes back to the kind of childhood my sisters and I had. We had a wonderful, loving support system growing up. We didn't have money, we certainly weren't indulged in any way, and we never felt entitled to anything. But if things had been awful at home, if our parents had been troubled and full of bitterness at their fate, if drugs or alcohol had poisoned the atmosphere, then any one of us might have wanted to leave and never come back. Thanks to God, that didn't happen. We're all three here because of the good times we had, because of the memories and the love we shared and continue to share. All of that is irreplaceable and everlasting. So why would we ever want to leave?

I go away from here a lot—in the heyday of Alabama we were on the road sometimes for 250 to 300 days a *year*—but when I come back, it is ultimate reality. At least it's *my* ultimate reality, and I don't see that changing any time soon.

Plus, you can't beat a life centered on soul-stirring Southern gospel music.

# CHAPTER 2

# GOD AND MUSIC

*We sat down at the table and thanked God in prayer*
*Cause we had plenty to eat and plenty to wear*
*We had patches on our britches but Momma kept us neat*
*We had food on the table and shoes on our feet*

"FOOD ON THE TABLE" BY RANDY OWEN

The four constants in my life, then and now, are, in no particular order—work, faith, family, and music. And they are all deeply intertwined. The music I write and perform is largely about work, faith, and family. The music I was raised on was largely the rich Christian tradition of Southern gospel music. In the late 1960s, my parents and sisters formed their own gospel group, the Owen Family, and played together for the next twenty years. As a kind of coming-home gesture, I guess, the last two original Alabama albums at the time of this writing were both made up entirely of inspirational music, most of them songs my cousins and I have known since we first learned to carry a tune. It was like coming full circle, musically.

Faith is at the root of all this. My sister Reba, a very devout woman, probably puts it best. Ask her about anything to do with her life or my life—my success, talent, good fortune, and overcoming some difficult times—and her answer will be pretty much the same: "It's God," she'll say. "Because He is in charge. He is in charge of everything that happens in our lives. You have to go on faith and trust that He knows what He's doing. And it's in the asking. If you never ask, you aren't going to receive what you want and need. The Bible says He will supply your needs if you give Him honor."

There is a favorite family story that we all like to recount to drive this point home. When Reba and I were in grade school, we drank water out of an old well at school, a pretty common thing back then. Apparently the sewer system had backed up into the well water and contaminated the system with bacteria. A lot of kids got hepatitis, including Reba and me.

I was especially affected, and everyone in the family thought I might not make it. Mama and Daddy didn't rush either of us off to the doctor's office. In that day and time, it simply wasn't their first impulse. Doctors were expensive—health insurance was unheard of—and they had little contact with them. They weren't opposed to organized medicine—it was just unfamiliar to them.

Their first impulse was to pray. My aunt Lillie and uncle "H." came over and prayed for us. At the time, I hadn't eaten anything for two or three days. The whole family prayed hard, then took a good long look at me and said, "Randy, do you think you could sit up and eat some ham?" And I said, "Yes, I believe I can." I still felt sick as a dog, but I got up out of bed and started eating the cured ham they were serving up. And I never went back. Almost instantly—miraculously—I was over the hepatitis and have never been that sick since.

When something like that happens to you, in that kind of miraculous way, it gives you faith. We all believed then, and continue to believe, that God healed me that day. It took Reba much longer to recover from her sickness. If you asked her today, she'd tell you that at the time, she didn't have as much faith as I did. She was weak, she'll say, and only later did the Lord intercede and strengthen her faith.

To this day I still wonder what might have happened if the family hadn't gathered in prayer for my recovery and I hadn't gotten out of that bed to eat a little ham.

This may sound corny, but I sincerely believe, and have since that hepatitis incident, that God has had his hand on me, protecting me in some way and directing me to do His work, however badly I might stumble through the assignment. Like millions of people, I pray every night, and I'm proud to do it. I go to the local Methodist church every time I can for one simple reason—going to church for me is a soothing, reassuring experience. It's a special place, and as long as it's Protestant, I can understand what's going on. I really don't know much about other churches, which doesn't mean I'm wrong or they're right. You can get up and leave an address or a location, but it's hard to leave a culture.

I don't practice religion with the same rigor and devotion as my mama and my two sisters, but I do think I practice it in a practical, hands-on way. I try to direct at least part of my daily life toward the needs of others. That might be my kids, my wife, my many relatives, or the much larger family of the St. Jude organization and other worthy charities. If I have a personal ministry, it is in the charity work I do, from St. Jude to helping young farmers-to-be in Alabama get a foothold in life, and the older I get, the more that kind of work means to me.

And the sense that God has a hand on me and I'm in His presence doesn't leave me when I'm out on the road or otherwise absorbed in the day-to-day business of making music. Reba likes to recount the dozens of times I'd be about to go onstage and I'd call Mama and say, "Mama, it's really stormy and dangerous here. I need you to pray that the weather lets up." And sure enough, more than once, the weather would clear so we could perform. You tell me that Mama's incessant prayers for our safety and well-being didn't matter.

Being constantly on the move, constantly overwhelmed by all the energy and excitement that goes into performing before fifteen to twenty thousand people every night, can easily leave you in a never-never land somewhere between the show world and the real world. You often don't even know what city you're in, like you're helplessly wandering around in some altered reality of backstage dressing rooms. Amidst all that chaos and madness,

I've never really felt alone. I certainly have my parents, and my parents' faith, to thank for that.

My daddy had a similar health crisis as my hepatitis when he was thirteen, in the early 1930s. He caught pneumonia, a very bad case, and given the way his family lived in those days—poor, self-sustaining farmers far out in the country—they didn't exactly rush him to the local ER. On the most critical night of his illness, a large group of family and friends formed a prayer vigil outside the farmhouse and prayed all night for his recovery.

Meanwhile, inside, his own mother, my grandma Owen, spent the night rubbing his chest with coal oil. I guess it worked something like Vicks VapoRub does today, as a topical salve that had some effect on easing the pneumonia. Either because of the intense prayer, or the coal oil, or both, my daddy survived the night and slowly recovered. Along the way, unfortunately, his heart and lungs were damaged.

Later on Daddy was turned down for service in World War II because of his damaged heart. He tried to make up for that by growing as much corn and cotton as he could to help the war effort. When I was a youngster, he decided that his impaired health dictated that he stop smoking. This was long before 12-step programs and Nicorette gum. I remember vividly the day he took a pack of Winstons out of his pocket and placed it on the mantel above the fireplace.

"That's it," he said, "I have officially quit."

That pack of Winstons stayed up there for years, and he never smoked another cigarette. Given all the trouble most people have stopping smoking, the older I get, the more astounding I find it that he had the ability, the willpower, to just up and quit, and quit for good.

Health matters aside, faith's deepest connection in my boyhood was with music. Faith and music were two sides of the same coin. As I described, Mama and Daddy played and sang together from the moment they met. Daddy had a sister, Lela, and the three of them were performing at sing-ins and tent meetings. Church music was simply a part of my family's collective DNA.

First in church, at weekend sing-ins, and in the family living room, then later on radio, and finally on TV, white gospel music was always in the air. Back in the days of black-and-white TV, if you got the antenna turned just right, you could see classic groups like the Spear Family and the Singing LeFevres perform Southern-gospel music on Sunday afternoon out of, say, a station in Atlanta. That was a big deal in my household—a group of people, mostly kinfolk, gathering around a static-filled black-and-white TV screen to watch this music, in the same way people in the '50s in New York City probably gathered around to watch New York–based shows like *I Love Lucy* or *The Honeymooners*. As a little kid, I vividly remember that Eva Mae LeFevre, the wife of Urius, sister-in-law of Alphus, was the piano player for various incarnations of the group. In those days, she was the only female onstage, and she dressed much nicer than the men.

I don't remember seeing black gospel music on television, but you could hear it on radio, and my parents always spoke highly of it. To them, there were two kinds of church music: "proper" music, sung in perfect pitch, note to note, without deviating from the musical text; and music filled with spirit, infused with high energy and spontaneity, an uninhibited outpouring of the soul. Both black and white gospel music share this joyful exuberance. In many ways, they were much the same music, just sung in slightly different styles in two different cultural traditions.

My daddy was a born guitar player. That was his passion. Right before I was born, I'm told, he sold his favorite guitar for ten or fifteen bucks because they needed the money. I can't remember what age I was—probably around six or seven—but I distinctly remember his saying, "You know, I think I really need to get me another guitar." He did just that, and I sat at his feet, watching him play. He tuned his guitar in a funny way, a way I have never figured out to this day. Then he announced, "Well, playing this way is going to be much harder for you, son, so I'll tune it like everyone else does."

So he played whenever he could, and I soon became consumed with the thought of playing myself. It was all his fault, so to speak.

Daddy bought me a little acoustic guitar, called a Stella, and began to show me a few chords. The fact that I could pick the strings at all was something of a miracle itself, given a near-tragic accident that I had had years before when I was about two and a half. Daddy was driving a rental car while his truck was getting fixed, and when I got into it, I slammed the door on my thumb and cut the end clean off. I can't recall what happened after that, because I was in shock and later sedated, but Daddy rushed me to a local doctor who sewed my thumb tip back on. I spent the next year or so with a thumb brace so it could heal. Mama kept it clean and made sure I didn't overuse it, and my thumb eventually grew back into a functional digit. Without my daddy's quick action, that half thumb could have ended my guitar picking before I could write my name.

With all my fingers and thumbs, it didn't take long for me to learn the basics. It was crazy. As my mama would say, "It just come natural." Perhaps because, at the time, I was shy, isolated, and stuck close to home, I advanced so fast at basic guitar skills that Daddy came to me one day and said, "I'd like to show you more, son, but you're way past me already. So we'll just play together." For a preadolescent kid, it was a genuine thrill to be able to pick up a guitar and play alongside my dad.

I especially liked it when he bragged on me. The fact that he thought I had done something well meant a lot to me. Every performer, musician, actor, or stand-up comedian has a need to be recognized, to be *seen*. Given my incredible shyness, maybe I had even a greater need for that kind of public approbation. Especially if the public I was performing for was my daddy.

As I said, Daddy gravitated toward the guitar style of the great Merle Travis. Even early on, I felt inspired by a man who himself was inspired by Merle Travis: Chet Atkins. We all loved the close harmony of popular '40s and '50s gospel groups like the Louvin Brothers (from Section, Alabama), the Florida Boys, and the Delmore Brothers (from Elkmont, Alabama), not to mention the Speer Family (with the built-in-maybe family connection), the Stamps Quartet, the Lefevres, and a dozen more.

I remember one particular gospel song that my daddy just loved: a Florida Boys recording of "Daddy, Hold My Hand." We had it on a 33 that we got on sale down at Bargain Town in Fort Payne. I never saw it on another record. When I was producing the first inspirational music project for Alabama decades later, I thought seriously about doing that song, because my daddy had loved it so much. I even tried to track down Les Beasley, the lead singer and manager of the Florida Boys for forty-plus years and a major figure in spreading gospel music on television. By the time he got the message, unfortunately, the record was done, without that song. Maybe next time.

Daddy introduced me to secular country music as well. It was pretty much in the air we breathed in Alabama in the 1950s and '60s. After all, perhaps the greatest country singer-songwriter of all time, the great Hiram King "Hank" Williams Sr., was born in Georgiana, Alabama, and buried in Montgomery. He was an absolute hero to my daddy and most others in our area. Plus, the weekly broadcast of the *Grand Ole Opry* on WFM came from Nashville, only a hundred and sixty miles away.

One country song in particular that I associate with my daddy in those days is the Buck Owens mid-'60s classic "Love's Gonna Live Here." Daddy just loved that song. It had a special meaning to him that went far beyond just being a catchy country tune. Perhaps because of personal sorrows I knew nothing about, it made a deep connection.

Daddy kept farmer's hours and got up early, around 5:30 every weekday morning. His first assignment was to build a fire in the fireplace. It was our only source of heat. Later he taught me how to build the fire, but until then, I was usually tucked away and fast asleep and would be stirred awake by the crackling and popping of the wood as it burned and sent embers up the chimney. I didn't have an alarm clock. Those popping sounds were my wake-up call.

As the rest of us slept and that fire got going, that's when Daddy would get out his guitar and play. And after we got a radio, he would tune it in to listen to the local farm programs to find out the current price of hogs or what was going on in the corn market. Then he would find a country-music station or a show like *The Little Red Barn*—the theme song was "In a Little Red Barn (On a Farm Down in Indiana)"—on station WOWO, a clear-channel AM outlet out of Fort Wayne, Indiana, or something on WHO out of Des Moines, the same station that once hired Ronald Reagan to re-create Chicago Cubs baseball games. You could hear these faraway stations crystal clear at 5:30 in the morning. It was pitch dark outside, which added to the quiet and solitude of the situation—my dad, guitar in hand, sitting next to the light of an early-morning fire, thumb-picking and singing gospel tunes.

We all loved to hear Daddy play the guitar at any time of the day. To this day, Mama keeps his last guitar tucked away under her bed every night. She says it gives her comfort.

My radio tastes were a little different than Daddy's. I listened to everything. As you'll probably hear more than once in this book, I never wanted to sing. That was the furthest thing from my mind until my late teens. I just wanted to play the guitar. I didn't mind singing with the family—in the background—but when I was listening to my own brand of music and absorbing all the different riffs of popular music, I was focused on guitar picking.

As for the popular country music of the time, I just idolized Merle Haggard. Even at a pretty young age, I could hear the deep conviction in his voice and knew he was an incredible songwriter. Songs like "Sing Me Back Home" and "Today I Started Loving You Again" evoked real life much more profoundly than most popular music, country or otherwise. But I was far from immune to the pop hits of the day, from "Sugar Shack" by Jimmy Gilmore and the Fireballs to anything that came out of Elvis Presley's mouth.

After we got a radio in the house, I couldn't wait to get home and turn it on and listen to Jett Fly (otherwise known as Tommy Jett) on WFLI out of nearby Chattanooga. It would be the full range of pop music, from the Four Seasons to Motown. And because it was AM, you could hear it loud and clear.

My early teens were also the period when pop music was getting ready for the British Invasion. If you paid attention, you started to hear the utterly fresh sound of British imports like the Animals, the Dave Clark Five, Peter and Gordon, and of course the Beatles and the Rolling Stones. It was entirely new, at least to my Southern ears: new attitude, new harmonies, new recording styles. And it all worked its way into the yet-undiscovered

Alabama style. I remember staying up late at night and listening to a show called the *British Countdown* out of WHK in Cleveland, Ohio, the future home of the Rock and Roll Hall of Fame. My parents, as far as I knew, weren't aware that I was listening to music like that.

As for the two powerhouse groups, I liked the Beatles more at the time, but today I'd have to say I find the Rolling Stones more compelling. My guess is, looking back, that the harmonies of these English rock groups had as much to do with the later harmonies of Alabama as did the country-gospel groups like the Louvin Brothers. It may all be part of a long continuum. Early on, the Beatles did covers of songs by the Everly Brothers, a country group very similar in sound to early gospel duos and quartets.

My second guitar was a Harmony Archtop and around the time I was listening to late-night radio, my daddy bought me a Supro electric guitar with a Premiere amplifier. It was beautiful—all white. I still have a picture of Rachel, Reba, me, and that guitar over Mama's piano but she won't part with it. It's the only such picture that exists.

As I worked to master it, I used to take that guitar and amplifier out to the front porch, turn the amp wide open, and play my heart out. You could probably hear my second-class rendition of Johnny Rivers' "Secret Agent Man" all over Lookout Mountain. Again, I never thought about singing—just playing that guitar. And, I swear, there is nothing in the world that sounds any better than the sound of a single electric six-string guitar being picked on a porch at night way out in the country. There was nothing going on out there soundwise other than a few crickets or cicadas. It was like the whole world came to a halt to hear you play that guitar. It was magical.

All of my family was involved in music in one way or another, but when I was about nineteen, Mama and Daddy decided to put together a formal gospel group, the Owen Family, and perform together on a regular basis. By that time Reba was married and out of the house, and I was pursuing my own eclectic musical tastes, so the original group was Mama on piano, Daddy on guitar, Rachel on bass guitar, and Reba playing tambourine and harmonizing.

Rachel, as I said, was much younger than Reba and I—thirteen years younger than I, eleven years younger than Reba. She started singing in church, she recalls, when she was about five and became the third mainstay in the Owen Family at age eleven. By then Daddy thought she knew all the notes well enough to harmonize with him. Daddy sang lead on almost every tune. Mama loved his voice—he could sing soprano or tenor and any kind of harmony. "If you could carry a tune," she said, "he could sing with you." He didn't sing bass, however. He apparently didn't have the voice for it.

At some point Rachel took up the bass guitar. Mama remembers going to work at one of the sock mills for two weeks to raise the funds to buy her an old red bass guitar and amplifier from my daddy's nephew Odis. Daddy was no bass player himself, but he taught her a few chords, and she basically taught herself from there on. She never had a formal lesson.

The Owen Family, once constituted, played for any local country church that asked them to play, and they played for free. They played mostly evening performances to an average crowd, according to Mama, of a hundred people or less. And over the years, every denomination of small church asked them to play. Daddy was quick to mention that they were once invited to a local Catholic church.

They traveled, usually in an old Chevy van, to locations mostly in Tennessee, Georgia, and Alabama. They worked their schedule around growing season, harvesting season, and other work. In those days they traveled to little churches often situated on poorly kept dirt roads—they didn't have the luxury of mud tires—and it rained a lot. More than once, they ended up in a ditch and someone would have to come along and pull them out. They probably never went more than seventy-five miles to get to a venue, but sometimes it took them quite a while to get there. And, believe me, there were—and still are—a lot of churches within seventy-five miles of Lookout Mountain. They were so busy at some points that they didn't have a chance to go to church themselves unless they were performing at one. They might play one function on a Sunday afternoon and another one forty miles away that evening. A family church they could call their own, at least during that time, was out of the question.

And they did it all for the Lord.

They saw it like a ministry, a ministry of music. They'd show up at a church or church basement, maybe get a little bite to eat if a potluck dinner accompanied their performance, then play

God's music. The only pay they ever received was an occasional love offering. They never set a price, but some churches, especially the bigger ones, might give them some money to pay for gas and other expenses. Reba remembers how flabbergasted they would all be if some congregation came up with a hundred-dollar payment. The work didn't fill their coffers. It filled their spirit.

Though she had a young family to raise, Reba would try to join the others at one of these sing-ins every chance she got. If it was any kind of special occasion, she'd be there and so would I. I was perfectly happy to stand in the back and add my guitar to the proceedings and occasionally join the harmony behind Daddy's lead with Reba or Rachel.

The Owen Family got around, that's for sure, and though my role in the group was anywhere from minimal to nonexistent, it doesn't stop people today from remembering it differently. Whenever I'm out in the world, someone will invariably come up, like a gentleman did recently in Montgomery, and tell me how much he enjoyed seeing me singing and playing with my family the time the Owen Family came to his small country church. As far as I could remember, I had never been to his church, with or without the Owen Family, but I sure wasn't going to tell him that. I just swapped the titles of a few old gospel tunes with him—"Oh, yeah, we'd play that one every time we'd perform . . ."—and leave him with a fond memory of an area gospel group that he, and many others like him, obviously enjoyed.

By the time the Owen Family really got going, I was through high school and in college. There was a period when I joined up with another gospel group—called the Big Rock Singers—but the core group that became Alabama was already working for tips in Myrtle Beach, South Carolina, when Mama, Daddy, and Rachel were working every church in the greater tri-state Fort Payne area.

In the late 1970s—Rachel was fifteen at the time—Daddy decided it was time for the Owen Family to cut a record. We all got together on that venture. Simply called *The Owen Family*, it was a collection of gospel standards like the first cut, "I Am the Man, Thomas." Daddy sang lead on almost every cut except one where Reba sang lead and one where I did. I sang the lead on the old standard "Silver Headed Daddy of Mine," since it was a song about a son paying tribute to his dad. There is also an all-instrumental cut that showcases Mama's splendid piano playing.

Mama still plays every chance she gets. Besides frequent appearances at local churches like the Rainsville Community Church, the Adamsburg Church of God, Liberty Hill Baptist Church, where many of my kin are buried, and the Mount Carmel Wesleyan Church, she also plays at a lot of funerals. It is a wonderful thing to watch her play. She has this old spinet piano that she's had forever in her living room, surrounded by the same decor that's been there for decades. She'll walk out of her kitchen, take off her apron, and sit down at that piano to play a tune. Once her hands touch the keys, she is transformed. She plays with the spirit running through her veins, the same way she no doubt played that summer long ago when she played for the singing school where she met Daddy. Early on, I learned something from the way Mama played and her attachment to the gospel music that she joyfully performed. This was not just entertainment for a crowd. This was food for the soul. I felt the same way when Alabama later recorded those two inspirational records. They both connected me to the earliest music in my life. Plus, those records brought a smile to my mama's face.

My daddy never made any money from his musical endeavors. He never became a gospel star or went on television or was asked to perform on one of the Gaither Homecoming Tours. But I'm pretty sure he dreamed of becoming a commercial success as a singer and guitar player. He loved recording the Owen Family album, and whenever there was an opportunity to play live on a country radio station, he was there. He was a born performer, and he played that urge out as best he could, mostly for love offerings and the gratitude of area country people. He certainly passed that spark of ambition on to me.

On the other hand, I think a lot of my own ambition came from the inside, not from an outside role model like my mama or daddy. I was born with it, I think. When I was growing up, I never felt like I quite fit in. I never fit in with the guys who went around drinking and partying and starting fights and often ending up in jail or worse. And I didn't feel too comfortable with the idea of simply following in my family's footsteps and continuing to work as a small farmer. I love the farm life, that's for sure. I live on a farm today—more of a ranch, actually—raise cattle and chickens, house three horses, and tend a lot of land. I've never had a strong desire to live anywhere else, or in any other way. But growing up, I felt restless and often unsatisfied. I had a deep urge to do more.

There seems to be one like me in almost every family—one who hears the faint beat of a different drummer and decides to follow it at a very early age. The restlessness was not an indictment of rural life. Just the opposite—it was a desire to celebrate that life on a much larger stage.

Simply put, I wanted to be somebody. From the time I was a small child, I tried to do everything I could to please my mama and daddy and make them proud. My mother, a very bright woman, started homeschooling me when I was three because I had an intense desire to learn. By the time I got to the first grade at the Adamsburg Junior High School, I was bored. When I got to the second grade, it was only a few days before the teacher, a very pretty, slender woman named Mrs. Blake, called my mama in for a consultation. I thought I was about to get punished for being so antsy and talking too much in the classroom. No, I was being moved ahead to the third grade. All this meant in those days was moving from one side of the classroom to the other, but it was a big move, and I could tell how much it pleased my mama.

I had big dreams, probably from the first time I played guitar next to my daddy. And I took those dreams seriously. Later in high school, for instance, I made a conscious decision not to have a serious girlfriend. I chased girls just like the next guy, but I worked at avoiding a situation where I'd get so hooked on a girl that we'd get married and settle down. That was a pretty common scenario where I came from—get married around seventeen or eighteen, go to work to support a family, have a crop of kids, and try to stay one step ahead of the bank.

I knew that was not what I wanted to do. I don't know why I knew that, but I did. I didn't want to find myself with a young wife with small-time dreams, someone who had never given a thought to shooting for something beyond the ordinary and everyday. I was turned off by that outlook. I pretty much kept my ambitions to myself, so it wasn't a source of tension with others. I never acted like an uppity outsider or music-star-in-training. I just didn't want to make any serious missteps that might stymie my dream.

I think that attitude really helped me to focus on pursuing my own goals and perhaps stay away from people who wouldn't be good for me and the life I wanted to live. If the hard rules of Christian living that my parents practiced taught me anything, they taught me discipline. And I think I set out pretty early to honor their influence and example and give them something back.

So if I was driven to succeed in the music business, I was driven both by that dream and by the desire to be able to do something for my parents and other family members. I don't really think I was driven by wanting to get out of poverty, and I certainly didn't just want to be able to give my loved ones money or material things when they needed them. To this day, my mama turns down virtually everything material I offer her. It's more than money. It's the ability to make a phone call and help them out of a legal jam, like that incident in my boyhood when my daddy was accused of trading in stolen cattle and I felt he was being treated like a common criminal. Or, again in my daddy's case, to be able to take him on an airplane ride that he always wanted to go on. I like to be on top, but ego gratification was only a small part of my drive. I wanted to be somebody as much for my parents as for myself.

# CHAPTER 3

# COTTON DUST

*It was July hot 'cross Georgia*
*On my way to Myrtle Beach*
*I just got my diploma*
*so I set out in search of me*

"TAR TOP" BY RANDY OWEN

My parents weren't educated beyond the eleventh grade, and they never placed a premium on going to college and getting a degree. Given their background and the way they chose to live, schooling simply didn't rank high on their list of life achievements. They placed a much greater value on hard work, raising a family, and living a clean, moral, upright life. They were farmers, grounded in the strong faith and folk wisdom of their forebears who lived much the same life they did. Unlike my generation, they didn't fret much about where their kids might end up. They figured they'd probably end up staying close to home and doing pretty much the same thing and living pretty much the same life as they did.

But both of them, in their own ways, were able to convey to my sisters and me a love of learning and the power of words. When he wasn't working all day raising cotton and corn or trading cattle or picking at his guitar, my daddy loved to read and often read aloud to the rest of us. He would sit us down at night and read aloud from the Bible. He could make those stories of ancient Egypt and Israel come to life. I knew it was something special that he would take the time to read to us out loud, but I don't think I really appreciated it fully until I had my own kids. I've tried to pass on to them the sheer pleasure and impact of reading aloud, to themselves and hopefully to their own kids someday.

Daddy also loved to read poetry, especially the poetry of the English-American poet Edgar A. Guest, enormously popular at the time. Edgar Guest wrote poetry that millions of regular Americans enjoyed in the first half of the twentieth century, and especially people who weren't particularly schooled in the finer points of meter and rhyme. He was aptly called the People's Poet. My favorite poem is "You." His folksy, easy-to-grasp, plain-speaking poetry would show up in newspapers and books, plus he had a popular radio show in the '30s and even briefly had a TV show called *A Guest in Your Home* in the early '50s.

My daddy adored the vernacular verses of Edgar A. Guest. Those poems spoke of home, faith, and the simple pleasures of life and were filled with an infectious native optimism. Daddy kept his books around the house, books with titles like *All That Matters* and *Life's Highway*. One of his most famous books, *A Heap o' Livin'*, contains his classic poem "Home" that millions like Daddy loved to read and hear read. I'm sure many of you, if you were raised in the South or Midwest, have a grandparent who memorized this poem and maybe recited it around the dinner table. It opens with:

> *It take a heap o' livin' in a house t' make it home,*
> *A heap o' sun an' shadder, an' ye sometimes have t' roam*
> *Afore ye really 'preciate the things ye lef' behind,*
> *An' hunger fer 'em somehow, with 'em allus on yer mind.*

Listening to my daddy read poems like this instilled in me a love and appreciation of both poetry and words in general that I carry with me to this day. Even before I was conscious of my own passion for such things, I'd begun to write song lyrics in my head, lyrics that would later work their way into early Alabama songs like "Tennessee River" and "Mountain Music." The link between the words I heard read by Daddy and the words I would spend my life making up is undeniable. By the time I got to college, I was consciously working at writing my own poetry. That's why I majored in English.

As I mentioned, my mother started schooling me in the three R's when I was of the age we'd now call preschool. Since we had neither a radio nor a TV, reading books and listening to stories from my daddy and his friends were about the only ways I could learn about the world. Mama obviously did a good job of giving me a head start, since it led to the decision that I jump from second to third grade in elementary school. This seemingly minor event came back to help me through a critical passage later in my young life.

I loved school and did fairly well at it up through the eighth grade. No one thinks like this now, but in those days eighth grade was something of a turning point in many people's lives, much as graduating from high school and college are today. Many of my cousins didn't finish high school—they just went to work on the farm or in a trade and never looked back. Since I was a bit of a country creature like they were—or at least that's the way a lot of kids with more money and better clothes saw us—I looked around at my friends and kinfolk and decided to do what they did—drop out of school.

I was fourteen at the time, having just completed the eighth grade at Adamsburg Junior High, when my daddy got sick from some unknown cause. He had been doing the relentless job of growing, picking, and marketing corn all by himself for years, and he had nobody around to jump in and help him out. It killed me, as his only son, to see my daddy hurt, and it hurt even more when he was helpless to do the most important job to keep the family going—farming corn. So I made the decision to drop out of school and do it myself.

At that point, we had a hundred and some acres of corn, most of it on rented land and ready to be picked. So while the other kids went back to class, I picked the corn, shoveled it into the truck, and hauled it off to the marketplace to sell. While that had been a tough job for my father, it was doubly tough for a fourteen-year-old working out in the field on his own. The corn was green, and the shoveling was especially backbreaking work. You grow up fast doing hard labor like that.

A near tragedy took place in those fields—I almost got my right hand cut off when I caught it in the old corn picker we had at the time. How it got stuck in there, I can't remember, but within seconds one of those blades would have come around and lopped it clean off. Fortunately, I jerked it out instantaneously, suffering only a ripped-off fingernail, or I would have never played the guitar again.

The corn got harvested and marketed, and I stayed out of school for about a year and a half, working alongside my daddy after he got back on his feet. It was a good life, as far as I could tell. I could work with my daddy, play guitar with him, and have a lot more time to hang out and hear his stories. And it might have stayed that way if I hadn't decided to get a summer job down at the junior high school. I was working around the school as a caretaker to make a few extra bucks, when I bumped into the principal, Mary Ellis. She was a beautiful, red-headed woman with a deep Southern accent. For reasons I will never quite understand, she took an interest in me and began to look into my school records.

She said, "Randy, I went back in the files and checked your grades, and you made great grades! You even skipped the second grade and moved right into the third. Why aren't you still in school?"

I had no good answer for her—I think I tried to explain that none of the other people in my family continued on in school and that at one point my daddy really needed my help—but she wasn't buying any of it. She insisted I try to get back in school, if I wanted to, and assured me I wouldn't have any trouble. I was more than a little worried. By that point I had been out of school for almost two years. What if I couldn't cut it anymore?

Actually, when I sat down with the high-school principal to reapply to high school, he thought pretty much the same thing. He wasn't sure I had actually finished the eighth grade, and in any case, a year and a half had elapsed—I was now sixteen—and I was probably wasting both of our time. Maybe he didn't like the way I looked. At the time, I was dark—heavily tanned from being outdoors all the time—with a full beard and the body of someone used to physical labor. Maybe he thought I had already found my chosen career path.

When I took this message back to Mrs. Ellis, she was not happy. After she finished cursing him for his obvious by-the-book shortsightedness, she wrote him a letter and sent it over, special delivery, along with a full report on my grades from the first grade on. She told me to go back there and sign up again, and if the principal gave me any grief, she'd be over in his office in no time.

Where do angels like Mrs. Ellis come from? I had had some great teachers in junior high, but she wasn't one of them. She had no vested interest in my education. She just took a liking to me, for whatever reason, and by going to bat for me at that critical turning point, she changed my life forever.

So I reenrolled in high school in the second semester of that year, which meant I was at least a year or more older than anyone else in the class. And I was a little rough around the edges. I looked like a buffed-up field hand, and my hands were stained with "cotton dust." This was particularly embarrassing. Cotton dust is very fine and gets into the pores of your skin. You can't really wash it off. You have to sweat it out. If you sweat a little, your skin turns a brown/black from the mixture of dust and dirt. It looks like you forgot to clean up before coming to school.

And though I was still shy and self-conscious in my social interactions, I had developed the defensive attitude that comes with being a poor working boy in a classroom full of "city" kids. I was hard as a rock from working, and that helped give me a new-found meanness. I was just waiting for somebody to say something I didn't like so I could smack him in the head.

I guess I needed that surly chip on my shoulder to get me through that rough transition. I needed to feel that God had a special hand on me at the time. It worked. I wasn't afraid of anything or anybody. Bring it on, pal, and I'll eat your lunch.

So, like preparing to walk into battle, I walked into the school that first day, and someone told me to go to my homeroom. I didn't know what a "homeroom" was. I'd never been to one. Finally I found mine, and as I walked into the classroom and across the room, this big lug of a ninth grader was holding a pint-sized kid out the window, threatening to drop him from the second floor. He apparently found this entertaining, and there was no one else in the room who was going to do anything about it.

This was my battle, I guess. Without much hesitation, I walked over and said to the bully, "Put him back in here." He instinctively said, "No way." Then he turned, slowly looked me over, and finally said, "Who are you?"

"I'm the guy," I said, "who's gonna whip your ass if you don't put him back in here."

I had already committed mentally to following through with my threat, and I think the guy knew this. He picked the little boy up and set him back down in the room. The kid ran over and got behind me like I was his older brother, and the bully just sneered and walked away. I guess it was my initiation rite into high school. I was there to stay, on my own terms.

A short time later that same first day, I almost lost it again. When I came in that morning, I was chewing gum. My grandma Owen loved Beeman's chewing gum, and she would give us kids a block every once in a while as a big reward for completing some chore. My parents chewed gum, too, as a kind of breath freshener. Beeman's gum bordered on being a luxury in my house.

So, the young teacher strolled in, saw me chewing a big wad of gum on the first day of school, and said, "Hey, young man, what are you doing chewing gum in my classroom?" I answered, "It makes my breath smell better." The whole class broke out laughing, at my expense. Only a boy from the sticks would chew gum to sweeten his breath, they all figured. The teacher laughed too.

I was deeply embarrassed and ready to knock the guy through the wall. I was waiting, almost hoping, he'd pop off again so I could teach him a lesson. Teacher or not, he was making fun of me, and I hated it.

As punishment, the teacher decided I should sit in the very front of the class, right next to him, and for about two weeks he'd come in every day and sit down at my side. I kept waiting for him to say something I didn't like so I could settle the score. He didn't, thank God, or my high-school career would have been over in a matter of weeks.

My redemption came soon after when a wonderful teacher named Mrs. Biddle administered what was to be my first high-school test, a test I remember in great detail. It was on diagramming sentences. After the test was done and Mrs. Biddle had graded them, she came over to my desk and asked, "Mr. Owen, where have you been going to school?"

"I haven't been going nowhere," I sheepishly answered. Another big classroom guffaw.

"Well," she said, "just so the rest of you in class know, Mr. Owen made 99.5 on this test. And the rest of you flunked." Talk about a proud moment. From then on, I was no longer the gum-smacking country boy in the room.

Mrs. Biddle, Mrs. Landstreet, Mrs. Hawkins, Mrs. Mallory, Mr. Holtzclaw, Mr. Guice, Mr. Shipp, Mr. Roche . . . these names mean nothing to you, but they were some of the most important people in my life. Those caring, patient, encouraging teachers made a huge difference in my life at a very critical point. Outside of my parents, they were the adults who guided me into adulthood.

I was happy to be back in school and continued to set my educational goals higher and higher. I didn't want to be looked down at or made fun of because my hands were covered with cotton dust or my clothes were a little threadbare, and I figured the more educated I became, the less that would happen. My daddy, on the other hand, was sad. I had made the decision to go back to school without much prodding from either parent. I think it broke my daddy's heart because he'd had his buddy with him all the time, working at his side, swapping stories and easing his load, and now he was gone.

That was probably the last sustained period of time that my daddy and I spent together—after high school, I was off to junior college, then college, and only home for a month or two at a time. Then every summer, my cousins and I relocated to Myrtle Beach, South Carolina, to help get Alabama off the ground, and during the winters we worked hard elsewhere. For that reason alone, I'm so glad, in retrospect, that I quit school for that year so I could simply be with my daddy all day every day. I didn't realize at the time how little time was left for us to be together.

I spent a lot of time in high school around people who went looking for trouble, found it, and ended up on the wrong side of the law. For whatever reason, I sidestepped serious trouble. I had a sixth sense about when it was coming and when it was time to simply move in the other direction. Again, looking back, I felt like that hand of God was nudging me in the right direction. Or I was just damn lucky.

I wanted to play all sports in high school—that's a good way to stay out of trouble—but I never did get to play on any team but the baseball team. I was interested in sports like football and wrestling, but there was the inevitable conflict between practice time and working on the farm. Working on the farm always won out. Finally, I got to play organized baseball my senior year, for Coach Chambers, won a letter, and loved every minute of it. I think we won all of three games.

My cousin Teddy Gentry, grandson of my father's older sister, Ollie, grew up nearby, and we spent a lot of time together, often playing music with our other cousins or other family members. I didn't have a blood brother, but I had the next best thing.

By the time we were in our teens, Teddy, eventually the bass player for Alabama, was playing off and on with various rock bands in the area, bands with names like the Shifters and Bickerson Flash. At an early age, he was learning many of the cover songs we'd later play to survive as a group. I never met anyone in those days with whom I really wanted to play. I wasn't particularly interested at the time in learning to sound exactly like one of the Top 40 bands of the era. I'd occasionally play with my family and in other pick-up situations, but mostly I kept to myself, tried to learn more guitar skills, and took my first steps toward writing my own songs.

I kept getting encouragement to carry on with music, from my daddy, for sure, but also from other wonderful people like my cousins Sonny and Linda Reece. Sonny and Linda ran a nearby place called Bingham's Barn Dance, and all through high school and early college, they'd hire me to sit in with the house band—I played piano and organ—and sing a song or two. Like the caring teachers I had in high school, the Reeces kept nudging me in the right direction.

Another cousin of Teddy's and mine, a more distant relative, was a year or so ahead of me in high school and already an accomplished musician. He was more of a "city" boy; that is, he had grown up in metropolitan Fort Payne and not on top of a mountain. His name was Jeff Cook. Although I had never seen myself as much of a singer, let alone a lead singer, I ended up singing a song with Jeff's band on one occasion at a public performance at Fort Payne High School. I guess that was the beginning of the beginning.

Then one Sunday afternoon—I was eighteen at the time—Teddy and I decided to get together with Jeff at Jeff's house in Fort Payne. Jeff was definitely a step or two ahead of us—he had a little more money, a little more worldliness, and he was already married. I had brought along a song I had written. It was called "Jeannie Brown." It was a true life story about a girl, Jeannie Brown, whom I had gone with. But she'd pulled away, saying she didn't want to be pinned down. She wanted to get away and take a few risks. I guess you'd say the song was about our sad parting.

Anyway, the three of us fooled around on our instruments for a while and then played this song. To me, it was a real eye-opener. What was unique about the experience was that we were singing together on an original song, not some worn-out rock-'n'-roll or country standard. We were all willing to throw caution to the wind and do something all our own. So we continued to work it up and perfect it, and along the way we took the first tentative steps toward a musical bond and a shared musical vision that would continue for the next forty years.

Soon after that, we were calling ourselves Young Country. That would later change to Wildcountry and finally, inevitably, to Alabama.

First we had to decide who would play what. From the time my daddy had given me my first acoustic Stella guitar, I had considered myself a guitar player, a lead guitar player. That's what I did. Jeff had other ideas. He announced that he wanted to be the lead guitar player and that I could play guitar, but in a supportive role. I could also be the featured singer, but even at eighteen, I still didn't picture myself as the guy out in front.

In one of those decisions that you look back on and see as absolutely critical, I went along with the plan. Jeff would play lead, Teddy would play bass, and I would play what is generally known as rhythm guitar. I think I originally accepted that decision for what I thought was the good of the group, a group I wanted to be a part of. It ended up as a decision that allowed me to exploit my strongest talents as a singer-songwriter and allowed Jeff to exploit his obvious gift as a master guitarist, not to mention his chops on the fiddle and a half dozen other instruments.

This lineup went a long ways toward determining what later became the sound of Alabama. I evolved a style as a rhythm guitarist that depended heavily on what are known as bar chords. Bar chords are created when you hold a chord and you hit every note in the chord by playing all six strings at once. It was a sound I particularly liked—it was bigger and fuller than normal rhythm guitar picking—and I came to use it on virtually every Alabama song I played on. It was a full-throttle rock-'n'-roll approach to playing rhythm guitar, a long way from a more delicate kind of country thumb picking in the style of Merle Travis or Chet Atkins. I used a very thick pick. I wanted to hit those strings hard and make sure you heard every note slightly out of tune.

It all just evolved. I didn't take it off of a Rolling Stones record or anything. I thought it was a great way to support Jeff's intricate lead-guitar playing. Now Jeff or Teddy might explain it differently, but to me, that kind of rhythm style simply gave us a unique sound for a four-piece band, the three of us and the drummer.

But the real uniqueness of Alabama, if we can claim such a distinction, is the unison of all the players. It was never conceived of or organized as a lead singer and a backup band, the classic country arrangement at the time. It was three equal musicians playing together. I sang lead but only because, at least initially, somebody had to. The principle idea was that we'd each merge our particular musical personality and style into the whole and come out with a much greater organism. To me the "sound" of Alabama is me singing lead and Jeff and Teddy singing along, bolstered by their incredible musicianship. And that sound was there from almost the very beginning. Everything that followed for the life of the band was merely an extension of that basic arrangement tentatively arrived at on that first Sunday at Jeff's house.

It would take years, most of them performing as a group capable of playing any rock or country song out there, before all the various elements of Alabama's sound, style, and presentation gelled into something unique and permanent. I loved to play with these guys and felt that we might just have something in our combined talents, but I was still intent on finishing high school and going to college.

And I had to continually sidestep trouble. One tragic incident illustrates this perfectly. Not long after I graduated from high school, I was going to a nearby junior college and hanging out with much the same crowd as always. Early one evening my girlfriend at the time and I decided to drive out to a swimming hole in the area called the Blue Hole. When we arrived, we bumped into a couple of guys I'd grown up with. That particular evening, they seemed a lot more interested in my girlfriend than in me.

Something told me to get the hell out of there. On any other occasion we would have gotten out, gone swimming, and just waited for things to unfold. That night we left without much of an explanation and went somewhere else. Only a few hours later, as the whole town found out the next day, those two boys grabbed another couple, tried to kill the guy by slicing his throat, and raped the girl. Both survived, but not without deep scars. The two guys were quickly caught and sent to prison.

Why did I leave that night? I have no idea. They weren't drunk or on drugs or in any way threatening. They certainly weren't strangers. The situation just felt wrong.

I think there are two main reasons why I got out of adolescence without a long rap sheet. First of all, as I've said, it was God's mercy at work in my life. But equally important, I think, I didn't want to embarrass my mama and daddy or in any way add to their burden. Someone would try to start something, and before I jumped in and started swinging, I would ask myself, "What would Daddy think of this?" There was always that governor going off in my head, a kind of foreshadowing of the consequences of what I was about to do and its effect on my parents.

Plus, I wanted to end up on top, and for that to happen, I had to stay focused, stay the course. Getting carried away in some impulsive way to settle some grudge or to test the limits of the law was not part of the game plan. In the end, it was just common sense.

In any case, I was headed toward a four-year college degree. Having gone through the humiliation of going back to high school and being sneered at, I was determined to earn something that couldn't be taken away. Music was a passion, but certainly not a surefire career path for an eighteen-year-old from small town Alabama. I needed a Plan B. College would give me that.

I first enrolled in an area junior college, Northeast State in nearby Powell, now called Northeast Alabama Community College, as a way to gain some academic footing for my next step. It was one of the smartest things I ever did. First, it didn't cost that much. The state government had bolstered the junior-college system in Alabama, so it was a great entry point. Tuition was $67.50 a quarter, all in, and they had a special bus service to and from campus so you didn't need a car, which I didn't have. I worked it out so I could go to classes during the day and work at a sock mill on the third shift from 11:00 p.m. to 7:00 a.m. I was hired by this fine lady named Ida Goza, even though I didn't know much about socks. I took on the most complicated task of all, running and occasionally fixing the knitting machines.

While I was going to Northeast State, Young Country had its first "professional" outing. We competed in a talent show at Section High School in Section, Alabama, over in Jackson County near Scottsboro. I played a 12-string electric guitar, Jeff played a Fender, Teddy sat in on drums, and cousin Jackie played bass. The song we played was the Merle Haggard classic "Sing Me Back Home." We won first prize, a free trip to the Grand Ole Opry in Nashville. It was our first taste of public acclaim.

Soon after, I graduated from junior college and went on to Jacksonville State University in Jacksonville, Alabama. I ended up getting a B.A. in English with a minor in Spanish, but not without a few more twists and turns. Young Country by this time had become Wildcountry, and through a series of contacts, we found out about a gig playing for tips at a bar in Myrtle Beach, South

Carolina. I had a major conflict—on one hand I wanted to finish college, get a B.A., and not drop out just a few months before I was through. On the other hand, I wanted to get to Myrtle Beach and play with my bandmates.

I finally went to the president of Jacksonville State and explained my predicament. He asked me what I was going to do with my college education, and I said I was headed to the coast of South Carolina to play music every night in a resort bar. Though I'm sure he didn't think this was the best use of a degree from his fine institution, he allowed me to finish school and graduate in absentia. That was a very big deal to me. I now had my Plan B. I could always fall back on a career of teaching high school English or Spanish if the music business didn't pan out.

But for now, I was headed to the Bowery. Or, to quote the lyrics of my song "Tar Top" again:

> *In the Bowery hangs the memories*
> *Of dreams that still come true*
> *Every time I see the spotlights*
> *I'm one of the Chosen Few*

# CHAPTER 4

# THE BOWERY

*Well I'm hangin' out down at Sloppy Joes*
*They may doze but they never close*
*And them 'Bama Boys at the Bowery*
*They can't dance but they play for free*

"DANCIN', SHAGGIN' ON THE BOULEVARD"
BY TEDDY GENTRY, GREG FOWLER, AND RANDY OWEN

Myrtle Beach, South Carolina, is one of the prime locales along the eastern seaboard, where everyone from Michigan to Georgia comes to play. Just south of the North Carolina state line, it is situated in a wide cove, part of what is known as the Grand Strand, a stretch of wide, sandy beaches along South Carolina's beautiful coastline. There are plenty of surrounding golf courses, if that's your sport, but it's mainly a beachfront resort for millions of regular, hardworking vacationers. People with kids and a modest income can hop into the camper, drive from West Virginia,

Tennessee, or Indiana, park in an inexpensive camper lot, and have a relaxing three- or four-day seaside holiday. It has all the appeal of Hilton Head or Miami Beach without the pretense or expense. Primarily in the summer months, the place is packed with sunburned kids in cutoffs and flip-flops, looking for a good time.

The Bowery, a nightspot right on the ocean, was certainly a place they could find it. In the days when Wildcountry, a.k.a. Alabama, began playing there every night as the house band, it was a pretty colorful joint. The sign when you walked in read Be 18 or Be Gone. Two hefty bouncers would greet you at the door as you entered a dark, smoky room with a long bar on one side and an array of pint-sized ice-cream-parlor-style tables and chairs in the middle. There was a stage, complete with chains hanging down from the ceiling for on-stage dancers to use, but there was no room on the floor to dance.

It was loud in there. People came to the Bowery to drink beer, holler and scream, and forgot their problems waiting for them back in Knoxville or Charlotte. And they came to hear the music and see the ever-changing freak show of performers that would pop up around the band. First there was a long-legged acrobatic go-go dancer who would pull herself up the chains onstage and hang upside down to the song "Long Train's Runnin.'" Then Bouncing Betty, the world's largest go-go dancer, weighing in at around 350 pounds, would dazzle the crowd with her shaking and shimmying. After Betty did her workout, you might see a guy named Don't Cry Joe, an old-timer who worked at the club and loved to sing old drinking songs like "It's a Long Way to Tipperary." He was also skilled at chugging beer.

Before Wildcountry began playing at the Bowery, the star attraction was a lead vocalist named Jeff who had polio and performed with crutches. It was that kind of place—a home for unusual characters to gather and perform.

Bouncing Betty and the others would fill in when we took short breaks between our nightly sets at the Bowery. We arrived there in March of 1973 to play the summer season. Initially I played for two weeks, went back to college while cousin Jackie filled in for me, and then came back for good. We thought this steady gig would be a good way to earn a little money and have the time to hone our writing and composition skills. It turned out to be the hardest work any of us had ever done, outside of maybe picking cotton. We played every night, Monday through Saturday. Showtime began at 7:00 p.m. and ran weeknights until 1:00 or 2:00 a.m., with minimal breaks. Many times during holidays we'd play daytimes too. On Saturdays we'd start around 8:00 p.m. but end at midnight on the dot, because there were blue laws in South Carolina at the time that prohibited the sale of alcohol even one minute after midnight Saturday night. We'd crash on Sunday and had little appetite for getting together to write or rehearse our own material. Before we knew it, it was Monday again and time to start another long week of performing.

We played mainly for tips. We had a receptacle on the edge
of the stage called the "pee pot"—it was an actual vintage cham-
ber pot once used for middle-of-the-night emergencies. Patrons
would come and toss in some money either to make a request
or in appreciation of something we just played. A tip could be
anywhere from a quarter to the rare hundred dollar bill, the latter
usually coming from someone too inebriated to care. The Bowery
people hung a huge cowbell over the bar, and every time a waiter
or bartender would get a tip, they'd clang that bell and rev up the
crowd. Not that it needing much revving up. It was just another
loud noise in a very noisy, rowdy place.

We fielded every request for every song of every musical
genre known to mankind outside of opera and Gregorian chants,
I think. Conway Twitty, Marshall Tucker, Merle Haggard, ZZ Top,
the Doobie Brothers, the Commodores, John Denver, Jim Croce,
Bob Seger, the Eagles, Marty Robbins—the playlist was endless.
And as far as I can remember—and Kelly backs me up on this—
there was rarely a time when we couldn't play, or at least play at
playing, any tune thrown at us. The logic was clear: our assignment was to please that crowd. If they weren't happy, we wouldn't
get any tips. If we passed on playing "I Heard It Through the
Grapevine" or "Rockin' Pneumonia and the Boogie Woogie Flu,"
that might have been a couple of bucks down the drain and one
disgruntled customer. So we became an all-hits-all-the-time bar
band, and it turned out to be the best musical education we could
have possibly received.

The Bowery was our testing ground. My test was becoming a lead singer, the front man, one of the hardest things I've ever had to do. I wasn't the kid who sang the national anthem or recited the Gettysburg Address at the school assembly at age nine. I could sing, thank God, and the more I sang in the context of the group, the more I gained confidence that I wasn't making a complete fool of myself. But singing in your cousin's living room and singing before twenty thousand people who are expecting you not only to sing the song in key but storm out to the edge of the stage, jump around, and *entertain* them in every way are two different experiences. Going into it, I'm not ashamed to say, scared the hell out of me.

As we evolved, I began to realize that few groups with a bashful, head-looking-at-his-shoes lead singer make it to superstar status. I had to constantly remind myself of that fact as I slowly, painfully redefined myself from crack guitarist to principal singer. Necessity is sometimes the best way to help you get over your greatest fears. In this situation I had no other choice. It was sing or find another group where I could just play the guitar and hide in the shadows.

As a lead singer, I faced not only the fear-factor but also my concern that I not sound like a clone of some other country singer with a deep tenor voice like Merle Haggard or Hank Jr. My natural style of singing was much like Elvis. If you go back and listen to the earliest Alabama recordings, I sound a lot like Elvis did before he went into the Army. I worked hard to develop my

85

own style of delivery so when you tuned in to an Alabama song, you recognized my voice right away. I didn't want to sound like Elvis, that's for sure. There was already one Elvis Presley, and he was pretty well known.

One thing about singing that I later learned from the recently deceased country great Eddy Arnold was an invaluable tip for any performer. He said the secret to connecting to a crowd is to pick out someone in the audience and sing directly to that person. You can move from that person to another but not before you make him or her feel like you're singing, one on one, a song dedicated just to him or her. That tactic has always worked for me, especially after Alabama got big and audience members were singing the lyrics right back. Making direct personal contact is paramount. Thank you, Eddy Arnold.

The staging of the group, just like about everything else we came up with, was simply a natural outgrowth of the roles we each chose. The three original players were equals, so we lined up in a row on the stage. I have no idea why I ended up in the middle. When I look back, I think it was because on the left side, Teddy had a big bass amp next to him, and on the right side, Jeff had three or four amps he wanted close by. The drums took up a lot of space behind us, so the best place for me was in the middle. As many people have pointed out, this was the way a rock band tended to line up onstage, not a traditional country band. We probably realized that at the time, but it wasn't something we did to market ourselves as something different. It was convenient and it was the best arrangement for playing the way we played, no matter how you categorized it.

Another thing that began to define us early on was our look. For most of the history of country music, stars dressed up. What started out, at least for men, as string ties and felt cowboy hats evolved in the '50s and '60s into the elaborate rhinestone finery best exemplified by flashy Nudie outfits worn by Porter Wagoner. The women wore a lot of lace and crinoline, like Loretta and Dolly. If you were a country star, you dressed up. You were country royalty onstage, wearing clothes that dazzled and delighted the audience. I loved those outfits and the stars who wore them, but that was not my way of dressing.

We felt more comfortable in jeans and T-shirts, more like the appearance of the Marshall Tucker Band. We were never dubbed country "outlaws" like Willie Nelson and Waylon Jennings in their Saturday-night street clothes and long, stringy hair, but we were about as close to outlaws as you could be. We all kept our hair pretty long because that's the way we'd always worn it. I had no choice. If I cut my hair, it would grow back in three weeks. And coming from the bar-band venue of coastal South Carolina, we dressed like the people who were throwing us tips every night, who themselves dressed like every grungy rock-band performer since Keith Richards. If we performed in worn-out Levi's, that was fine with them. We just looked like another band, period. They were there for the music, not the style show.

Again, none of this was by design, but as we went along, it helped our audience realize that we had no intention of dressing above them and, by extension, performing on some star-elevated pedestal. Alabama has been called a lot of things in our time, but

87

no one has ever called us pretentious. Nor particularly offensive. We may have dressed like we just got out of bed, but we never fell down onstage in a drunken stupor or lit our guitars on fire or shouted obscenities to the back row. You could bring your folks to the show without fear of embarrassing or upsetting them, unless they were dead set against shaggy hair or secular song lyrics about making love.

The Bowery also allowed us to play our own original songs and actually "test" them out on an audience, in the same way a stand-up comedian will go to a small club and test comedy material before he does a routine on *The Tonight Show*. I remember playing the song "Feels So Right" to a crowd of women from Washington, DC, who were secretaries and aides to congressmen. I wasn't sure about one verse, so after the show, I polled them for their opinion. They said not to change a word, and I never did. I really miss that experience of crafting and recrafting a song as you sang it nightly to real people.

Dancing was not just discouraged at the Bowery, it was prohibited. If a couple got up to dance and took up much-needed room from other patrons, they were asked to sit down or get out. This no-dance policy dictated what and how we performed onstage. We weren't background music—we were the main entertainment, and we had to entertain. We couldn't get onstage and lean on a musical set of easy-to-dance-to tunes, like endless disco riffs. We had to put on a show, regale the crowd with their favorite songs, and keep 'em coming back for their whole stay in Myrtle.

We were essentially a country band dropped into an environment that favored R&B and rock-'n'-roll. When we could get our original tunes into the nightly mix, people responded to them even though they weren't a hard-country crowd. That told us something—that country music, done in a looser, more energetic way, could appeal to anyone who liked music, period. You could look like someone from the first row at an AC/DC concert and still appreciate and jump around to "My Home's in Alabama."

Our great friend and publicist Greg Fowler, Teddy, and I wrote a song later on that does a pretty good job of capturing the mood and spirit of Myrtle Beach in those days. It's called "Dancin', Shaggin' on the Boulevard." The shag, also known as the Carolina shag, is a swing dance invented in the Carolinas and is today the state dance of both North and South Carolina. It's a dance that fit the vibes of Myrtle Beach events like Sun Fun Week, which we also stuck in the song. We make reference to great groups like the Drifters, the Embers, and the Tams, not to mention some upstarts nicknamed "the Bama Boys."

> Got the top down and the traffic's slow
> It's Sun Fun Week and we all go
> Where the girls are sunnin' and they're lookin' good
> Well I never met 'em but I wish I could
> And we'd go dancin' shaggin' on the boulevard
> We'd go dancin' shaggin' on the boulevard

The great thing about the Bowery was that there was a completely different crowd every night. Because it was a tourist spot, people from all over the country came and went. It wasn't like playing at a local club and seeing the same people nightly asking for the same music. It was a cross section of America that came in to see us—all ages, all musical tastes. In some ways, it was an ever-changing microcosm of the audience that later made Alabama famous.

My wife-to-be, Kelly, was living in Columbia, South Carolina, when she first heard Wildcountry onstage at the Bowery. She was first attracted to our music—and later, I'm happy to say, to me—not because we played country music, but because we played R&B and soul music, her favorite music at the time. She loved to dance and taught dance and loved the rhythm of soul music. Hell, if we'd stuck to only country classics, she might have walked right back out the door.

For the next seven or eight years, the game plan was pretty well set. We'd relocate to Myrtle Beach in March of every year and start playing nightly as soon as we got there. We would be rooted there until after Labor Day weekend. Before most of us were married, we'd rent a big house with three bedrooms and plenty of other space and all pile in. We had a succession of five drummers over that period—among them, Ben Vartanian (BV in the song "Tar Top") and Rick Scott—who, for one reason or another, didn't work out for long. The group didn't find a permanent drummer until rock drummer Mark Herndon came out to hear us play one night at the Thunderbird Lounge in Florence, Alabama, in late 1978.

I tried to book gigs whenever or wherever I could—Holiday Inns, Ramada Inns, any small-time venue who would have us— but most of them occurred after Labor Day, during the winter season between September and March. In the summer of 1976, we had a disagreement with the management of the Bowery and decided to spend the summer in central Illinois. A club owner in the Champaign-Thomasboro-Rantoul area had three different places where he would book us. It didn't last too long. After only weeks, we'd been fired and were on our way back to South Carolina. We had to beg our way back into the Bowery. We were back at our home away from home.

The Bowery was the reason we ended up with the name Alabama. Over the years we more or less followed the catch phrases of country radio. When they called their music "Young Country," they were talking about us. We *were* Young Country. When they decided to turn up the volume on radio promos with "Wild Country!" we switched to Wildcountry. This is what we were called at the Bowery, though within a week or so after arriving, we took an Alabama sign already on the wall of the bar and put it behind us onstage. The Bowery wanted to appeal to the whole country, so they covered their walls with signs of all fifty states and the District of Columbia. No matter where you came from, you'd feel right at home.

So the Alabama sign soon became the way most people who wandered in would identify us. It wasn't like there was a splashy Vegas-style neon sign in front announcing "Wildcountry."

People from the state of Alabama tended to vacation in south Alabama, Mississippi, and Florida, so few bands from Alabama played in the Myrtle Beach area at the time, which made us stand out. People would say, "When is that Alabama group going to come back on?" or "Let's go hear those Alabama boys over at the Bowery." At some point we decided that actually calling ourselves Alabama was simply a good way of keeping our name out there, so we designed a distinct logo for ourselves that clearly distinguished the band from the state, and that was that. With a few modifications along the way, that's the logo we proudly carried with us for the next thirty-some years. The Bowery, in short, was the graduate school of American music for Alabama from 1973 until our last gig there on July 12, 1980. By that point we already had a hit record. And thanks to the Bowery, I already had me a wife.

Kelly Roseanne Pyle, soon-to-be Kelly Owen, my loving wife of the last thirty-three years, was an army brat. Born in Augusta, Georgia, the second child of six, she lived in six or seven states before she was fifteen, including Hawaii, as well as overseas in Germany. Her dad was a colonel with the 82nd Airborne, and they traveled to wherever the army wanted him. That itinerant upbringing couldn't have been further from the close-to-home, rural, Lookout Mountain upbringing I had. She had to adjust to new people and new situations almost every day of her life. She'd start the school year in Georgia and end it in Hawaii. She was much worldlier than I was, then and probably even now.

Her dad was based at Fort Jackson in Columbia, South Carolina, when Kelly, all of fifteen, and some friends—closely chaperoned by their mothers—came to Myrtle Beach for spring break. One mother heard that there was this really good band playing at this nightclub called the Bowery, so Kelly wanted to go. You had to be eighteen to get in, but this mother convinced the owner that Kelly just wanted to listen to the band and wouldn't touch any alcohol. So they let her in, closely watched, and she saw Wildcountry in our full glory.

Kelly remembers details of things like this that I've long for-gotten. "So I went in," she says, "and Randy was sitting on a stool in the middle of that little stage, and he was wearing this caramel-colored suede hat, playing his guitar. He had long, thick, solid black hair down to his shoulders and a black mustache. What im-mediately attracted me, besides the fact that he sounded so much like Merle Haggard, were his forearms and his hands. He has very large hands. And I thought, *man, this guy is muscular. He knows how to work*." The next time she came in, she says, we made eye contact, but then again, in a place full of beautiful young women in bikinis, I probably made eye contact with more than one girl.

Kelly went home to Columbia but was back two months later, right before the summer ended. She had gotten a job at the local Columbia Dairy Queen for $2 an hour until she had enough money to afford a return trip. She was still only fifteen, but even then, when she wanted something, she'd just go after it.

So back at the Bowery, she found a little chair right in front of the stage and planted herself in my line of vision. She can even remember what she wore the night I first gave her more than passing attention: a Hawaiian print dress that her mom had made for her. It was a classy little dress that did a good job of offsetting her age and the fact that she still wore braces. She says now that she was "infatuated" with me and just wanted to meet and talk. It took a few visits before I got the message, I guess. Men are often not the most perceptive creatures on the planet.

Even at the advanced age of twenty-three and being the front man and lead singer for a band that played six nights a week, I was still incredibly shy. If George Harrison was the quiet Beatle, I was the quiet Alabaman. Onstage, I was learning to do the job and enjoy it. Offstage, I was still naturally bashful and retiring. Kelly, of course, was anything but.

I finally devised a way to make contact with her. I'll let Kelly describe it: "I had just about given up on Randy. I figured I was barking up the wrong tree. Anyway, one night, one of the go-go dancers came up to me at the table and said, 'You know what? I feel like kicking your ass.' And I thought, *Oh, no, what have I done now?* She went on, 'I've worked down here at this Bowery all summer long, and I've tried to get Randy Owen to go out with me, but he won't, and now he sends me over here to ask you if you would like to go out with him. He's too bashful to ask you himself, I guess.'"

Kelly gave the dancer a big thumbs-up, and five minutes later we were talking. I had to ask permission of her chaperone to take her out soon after, and I had to lay out the details of where we would go and when we would get back. The following Sunday, my only day off, I took her to get some pizza, which she wouldn't eat because it would get stuck in her braces, then to see the movie *Walking Tall*. I finally got around to asking her how old she was, figuring early twenties at least, and when she said "fifteen," I got a little nervous and decided maybe it was time to take her home. She left to go back to Columbia the next morning.

In my mind, this was more or less a summer fling. I wasn't ready to get serious with this obviously vivacious, independent woman. She was so young, she couldn't even get a driver's license. She was still a junior in high school. Her parents were military people and weren't sure she should be dating anyone at that point, let alone an "older" man who made his living singing in bars. In any case, she wrote to me, I wrote back, and by the time I got back to Alabama after Labor Day, I had decided to go see her before she moved out of the country.

My cousin Jackie and I drove my yellow Camaro over to Columbia and met the family, excluding her dad, who was then stationed over in Germany. We met Kelly and her mom in a Kmart parking lot so we wouldn't get lost trying to find their apartment. Back at their place, I wrestled with her little brothers and sisters, and Kelly and I got to really know each other. I told her my game plan for life: by the time I was thirty, if the music thing hadn't turned into a record deal or something, I had the education to become a teacher and would probably do so. She in turn offered up her own view of the future. She said she loved to dance, wanted to be a wife and mother someday, and hoped to end up living in the country. Her grandparents lived on a farm in rural Georgia, and she'd always loved that life. All of this was pretty much what I wanted too. There was only one immediate problem: Kelly and her whole family were soon on their way to Germany for two years to be with her father.

I stuck around on that first trip as long as I could, taking her back and forth to high school and getting to know her mom and family as best I could. Her mother was obviously a strong, resourceful woman, taking care of six kids while her husband served the country in the military. It wasn't an easy life, but she handled it well. One morning right before I left, I got out my acoustic guitar because I wanted to play Kelly this song I had been working on for some time. It was a song about a girl back in Fort Payne I had liked a lot but with whom things didn't work out. I wrote the tune about how I felt about that girl back then, but I was singing it to *this* girl right now for whom, I was slowly realizing, I had much deeper feelings.

A few years later, the song became an early Alabama hit. It was called "Feels So Right." It opens with these lines:

> *Whisper to me softly, breathe words upon my skin*
> *No one's near and listening, so please, don't say goodbye*
> *Just hold me close and love me, press your lips to mine*
> *Mmmm, Mmmm, Mmmm, feels so right*
> *Feels so right*

Kelly remembers, "I started wiping the tears from my eyes, and I said to him, 'Let me tell you something. I don't know if I'll

ever see you again but I hope this is a No. 1 song for you someday. That is one of the most wonderful things that ever could be
said about a woman or said to a woman.'"

It was time for me to head back to Fort Payne that morning,
and as we walked to my car, I knew I had to say something now,
before we parted for who knew how long. Although she was all of
fifteen going on sixteen and knew she wasn't ready to get married
right then and there, I nevertheless had to broach the question.
"Would you, you know, ever consider, you know, maybe marrying me?" It wasn't a formal proposal, for sure. It was more like a
heartfelt stab in the dark. And Kelly said, "You know what? I sure
would. I'm awfully young still, but you have captured my soul,
not just my heart."

That was enough for me. We walked back in the house
to talk to her mama and let her know I was serious about her
daughter and she was equally serious about me. Her motherly
response was, in essence, "not so fast": "First of all, she's way
too young to be serious." According to her mom, Kelly got tired
of boys fast and would probably get tired of me. She went on:
"Also, she's off to Germany, so you'll just have to wait until we
go abroad and Kelly finishes high school." That would take a
while, she went on, and in those intervening years, anything
could happen.

So Kelly took off for Germany for the next two years. That
was a major test for both of us. Mrs. Pyle was right. Anything
could change. Kelly finished the last two years of high school,
went to German discos and danced with the local boys, and even

enrolled in business school so she'd know how to do something in the real world besides change diapers and clean house. I didn't give up, though, or get distracted by some other pretty girl who wandered into the Bowery. I made one or two ridiculously expensive long-distance calls from South Carolina or Alabama to Europe to talk to her, and it continued to feel right.

The following June, Kelly pulled a big surprise on me by coming back to the States unannounced to see me. All her girlfriends back in South Carolina, including the ones who were around when we first met in Myrtle Beach, had staged a car wash to raise the money to buy her a round-trip ticket. It was a wonderful reunion. Her girlfriends were right there in Myrtle to watch it all happen, like a real-life romance novel. Their pal Kelly had met the man of her dreams, a musician who might just make it big someday, and they wanted to be a part of it. The relationship was a classic attraction of opposites. I grew up bending corn and plowing mules, and she grew up on army bases, riding bicycles and climbing monkey bars. I was shy; she was brazen and headstrong. I'd never been more than two states away from home; she had traveled the world. Unlike the small-town girls with small-town ambitions that I tried to avoid growing up, this was a woman who shared the same big Technicolor dreams that I had.

It was awfully hard to say goodbye to her yet again when it was time for her to return to Germany. Kelly says it was the hardest goodbye she ever had to give, outside of the time she had to say goodbye to her dad when he took off to fight in Vietnam. In any case, the way I channel sorrow is through music, so after she left, I sat down and wrote another song. It's called "Goodbye (Kelly's Song)." I kept the song in my notebook of songs for years before Alabama could finally record it and do it justice. It's a very important song to me. I wrote it for Kelly, but many years later I ended up singing it as a solo at the funeral of my very good friend, Dale Earnhardt. In part, the lyrics I wrote at Kelly's and my parting go like this:

> *Before I fly and wave goodbye*
> *I say to you "Days with you are the best years of my life"*
> *But if I don't see you anymore*
> *Keep my words safely stored*
> *And I'll be back I promise once more*
>
> *Goodbye, goodbye*
> *Till I see you again*
> *Goodbye, goodbye*
> *I'll love and I'll miss you till then*

After a few months I got on the phone one day with her father, a man I had never met in person, and asked him for Kelly's hand after she finished high school. He said yes. I guess by that point both of her parents got the idea that Kelly wasn't going to lose interest in me and I wasn't going anywhere either.

We got married just as Kelly turned seventeen and I was twenty-five. Here's how we pulled it off: Kelly was back in the States now, and since neither of us knew the other's extended family that well—I still hadn't met her dad—we thought about having a wedding that would include everybody. Kelly had moved into my parent's house in Fort Payne, and following the strict rules of the times, when we said goodnight every night, she would go one way, and I would go the other. Then one day Kelly said, "You know, I've been waiting to marry you, and I'm getting a little tired of this arrangement." So we changed plans and decided to get married before a justice of the peace. Because Kelly was under eighteen, I had to get written permission from her dad for the proceedings. When it arrived from Germany, we took off to find a marrying judge.

Taking Mama with us as a witness, we got in the Camaro three days before Valentine's Day—February 11, 1975. I had to work on Valentine's Day itself. We headed for a justice of the peace in nearby Trenton, Georgia. It was bitter cold outside, I remember that. Before we could go into the courthouse, we had to go across the street and have our blood checked to make sure we weren't carrying any diseases. As we finally entered the courthouse, I told Mama to stay put until we went in and found out what exactly was involved.

The justice, Judge Gray, well into his seventies and having done this more than once, just started right in. He told me to stand here, Kelly to stay there, and began with his set speech, directing us in the vows of marriage. It was a very emotional moment. We had waited for this and didn't want to wait another minute.

We had already made a trip to Martin's Jewelers in Fort Payne, a business that is still thriving, and got a deal on the rings—one man's wedding band, one woman's engagement band,

and one woman's wedding band for $199.99. We exchanged rings and kissed; I slipped the judge $20, and as we headed for the car, we realized we had left Mama sitting there! It had all happened so fast, and we were punch-drunk with love. She was a little taken aback. "But, why didn't you call me to come in?" she asked. I said, "Mama, the judge just started up, and we were halfway through the ceremony before we knew it, and we were in a hurry, too, so we just did it." That was a Monday. I had to be at a nightclub on Friday night. We had to get going.

The first night of our honeymoon was spent in a Motel 6 in Montgomery, Alabama—Kelly was still under 18, so she got to stay for free—and our first meal as newlyweds was a Whopper at Burger King. We went from there to Panama City, Florida, for three days, and then I dropped Kelly off at my folks, and I went back to work. Our life together was starting out in much the same way it would continue for the next thirty years.

Kelly moved in with my parents because it didn't make sense to put her into an apartment in an area where she'd never lived while I was on the road so much. Since both of my parents worked at the time, she'd try to help out as much as she could, like fixing dinner when they came home. It's not as if we had a lot of belongings to crowd into their house, so we didn't feel like we were imposing. Kelly never owned even a wedding dress, let along a large wedding trousseau. Kids today, like our recently married son, Heath, and his new bride, Cara Hudson, are given showers where they get silk linens and sterling silver and espresso coffee-makers. Our wedding haul amounted to a couple of Pyrex dishes and some Tupperware. Not that we complained. In fact, Kelly still has some of that Pyrex today.

From the moment we were married and had our abbreviated honeymoon, Kelly understood something intuitively that many young wives might have to struggle to accept. If I had any chance of making it in the music business, then one basic rule applied: the music came first. That didn't mean that I loved her any less or, as the years went by, that I loved my kids any less than a stay-in-town dad. It simply meant I was embarking on a demanding and unpredictable course in life, a profession that didn't always make allowances for anniversaries or birthdays or a two-week vacation in Panama City. This wasn't a lifestyle to me. This was a way to make a good living. I wasn't in it for 3:00 a.m. room service in expensive hotels and meeting groupies after the show. I was in it to make good music and support my family.

I had to get on a bus or van and take off thousands of times in our marriage, but what I wanted from Kelly, and she so lovingly provided, was a home to come back to. I wanted a place where I could be sure that every day when the kids came home from school, someone they loved would be waiting to greet them. At times it would be hard—very hard—for her not to get down and feel deprived and put upon in my absence. Raising three kids isn't easy even when both parents are around all the time. It's an even tougher job under the circumstances we faced, and it takes just the right person to pull it off. Thank God I found that person in that bar in Myrtle Beach early in my life.

Alison, the oldest of our three children, was born on December 13, 1977, which just happens to be the very same day on which I was born. We weighed the same, were the same length, and were both born in Fort Payne. I don't really know the cosmic significance of that, but it's easy for me to remember her birthday.

Anyway, the three of us settled into a trailer in Myrtle Beach, and the work of Wildcountry/Alabama forged on. Besides Myrtle Beach, we also had winter-season gigs that helped keep money in our pockets. There was a little club in Greenville, South Carolina, called Chief's Restaurant and Lounge—run by two diehard supporters and friends, Chief Jordan and Billy Bullock—that gave us steady employment between Labor Day and springtime. We also played at a club called the Split Rail in Winston-Salem, North Carolina, and the Brewery in Knoxville. No wonder we later built the Alabama Theatre in Myrtle Beach and consider all of the Carolinas like a second home. The whole region kept us alive for almost a decade.

Staying in one place for so long and building a solid, always-revolving fan base gave us a definite leg up when we began to record our original music. There was a whole underground of people around the South, people of all ages, who had heard about or had seen Alabama at the Bowery and would go home and tell their friends. Many successful rock bands—Bob Seger, Dave Mason, even Bruce Springsteen and the E Street Band—built on a base of live performances in their home region to generate multiplatinum records. When we arrived in Nashville, we may have been new to the kingmakers there, but a whole lot of regular people already knew who we were.

We actually recorded three albums before we finally signed with RCA Records in 1980 and released the album that put us on the musical map. The records were, in order, *Wild Country* (1973), *Deuces Wild* (1977), and *Alabama 3* (1978). A label called GRT released a single called "I Wanna Be With You Tonight" in 1977. It made it onto country radio and even broke the Top 80 on the music charts, but it wasn't a smash hit by a long shot. It hung around at the bottom of those charts for the longest time. It may have set a record for the longest song stuck at position No. 99.

The GRT contract, a one-record recording pact, was engineered by a man named Dick Heard whose company, unfortunately, didn't work out. We then decided to record our own album and pay for it, plus we needed to come up with some funds to buy our drummer at the time, Bennett Vartanian, out of his part of the contract. Jeff and I had to mortgage our cars. I took out a secured loan on my trusty yellow Camaro, and Jeff did the same with his 1972 Buick. Teddy, unfortunately, didn't have anything to hock, but we didn't hold it against him.

It was after this financial finagling to pay off our drummer that we made a telling decision. Jeff, Teddy, and I agreed never to bring in another partner or coequal member of Alabama, ever. The group would belong to the three of us, and that was it. It would be our name on the contract and no one else's. And that's the way it still is today.

The next big turn in the road was signing a management contract with a man named Larry McBride, a decision that turned out to be a colossal mistake. Mr. McBride took a song we had self-produced, "I Wanna Come Over," and got it released on a small label out of Dallas called MDJ Records. Through MDJ, "I Wanna Come Over" reached No. 33 on the country charts. In 1980, our signature song, "My Home's in Alabama," off the same record, broke the Top 20.

To make the long and frustrating McBride story short, after we signed a record deal with RCA Records and started making some noise, we began the laborious process of extricating ourselves from our management situation. It took us a lot of time and a lot of money—almost $2 million when all the dust settled—before we succeeded in getting out of that arrangement. When I look back upon that period, I'm almost bitter about this contractual entanglement and the stress and pain it caused in all of our lives. But we survived it, thank God, or I wouldn't be here today telling you this story.

Musicwise, what happened was that the same MDJ album, called *My Home's in Alabama,* was bought and rereleased on RCA Records, and if you read the fine print, it lists the producers as Alabama; our dear friend and record producer Harold Shedd; and Larry McBride. If you look in old record bins at flea markets today, you might be able to find a copy of the album on MDJ and another copy on RCA. Alabama's first two No. 1 hits, "Tennessee River" and "Why, Lady, Why," came from that record.

Around the time we were making *My Home's in Alabama*, two people entered our lives who became essential to our success. One was Barbara Hardin, the woman who booked the band almost from day one, and the other was Dale Morris, the manager who took our career from zero to a hundred almost overnight.

To hear them tell the story—and I trust their memories more than my own—it all started when Harold Shedd made a tape of our album and passed it along to his friend Dale because he thought Dale would appreciate this exciting new group he was working with. Dale, who I'll talk about more in a minute, then passed the tape on to Barbara, who had been working for him in various administrative capacities for the previous three years. Barbara was a Nashville native who had worked for an agency owned by Conway Twitty and Loretta Lynn before coming to work for Dale. She was in her twenties and looking for something to put her career in high gear.

Barbara started listening to the tape and couldn't stop. She claims to have played it over and over for three or four straight hours. She walked into Dale's office the next morning and announced that she wanted to become a booking agent and that she wanted her first booking act to be Alabama. At the time, Barbara worked in country but rarely listened to country music at home. She was a rock-'n'-roller by taste. She is not the last person who would claim, "Until Alabama, I didn't even like country music!" Every time we heard this, we knew we might just be onto something.

Soon after, Barbara, as probably country music's first full-fledged female booking agent, began booking us with Mr. McBride still as our manager, and as our relationship with him grew worse, our relationship with her grew more intimate. She became a sympathetic ear to our many complaints about how we were being handled, or mishandled. We had made no money in producing the record with him and barely survived on our cut of the stage shows. We were getting nowhere fast. She would ask Dale, already a very successful manager in the music business, for his arm's length advice and pass it on back to us. We soon realized that Barbara and Dale were people we could trust and work with for the long haul.

There is more to the McBride fiasco, but like I said, I am good at blocking out bad memories, and this was one of the worst. After we broke off with him, McBride got into some serious legal trouble, and around 1980 he ended up going to prison. Even though we were pretty burned out with managers by that point, it became increasingly clear that we needed a steady, creative hand to help us navigate the jungle of Nashville, and Dale Morris was that hand. It was probably the smartest business decision we ever made.

By late 1979 or early 1980, things started to feel like they were definitely moving. Barbara now had her hands full booking us into clubs outside of our usual stomping grounds. The MDJ edition of *My Home's in Alabama* was getting some notice and some chart action. After years and years of relative obscurity or at least a low-key regional reputation, we were finally getting national attention. A big, big turning point came in the spring of 1980 when Barbara booked us on the New Faces of Country Music Show, a showcase for emerging talent that was part of an annual Nashville event called the Country Radio Seminar. Reba McEntire, also just starting out, was on the same bill. It was a big gig for both of us.

The Country Radio Seminar, or CRS, is a big doing in the country-music business and has been since it began in 1969. It's essentially an around-the-clock, three-day cocktail party for country-radio personnel and country performers to rub elbows and exploit one another. Radio programmers from all over the country converge on Nashville to meet artists, established and new, get to know them up close, and get them to tape promos like, "Hi, I'm George Strait and you're listening to my favorite station in Birmingham!" Many fresh new country stars first meet the radio people who are so important to their rise at the New Faces Show. Tim McGraw, Kenny Chesney, and, of course, Reba are all former New Faces.

We got to our big New Faces showcase, and the people who ran it, steeped in an old style of country performing, made us do it their way. They wouldn't let us use our drummer because they had a studio group playing all the instruments. The three of us were forced to perform "My Home's in Alabama" without instruments, like we were a traditional country male trio. The guys in the house band had no idea how to play our music according to our arrangement, and the arrangement of Alabama music, then

and throughout our long career, was always as critical to the feel
of the song as the melody or the lyrics.

It was a nightmare. Teddy tried to show the house drummer
exactly how to play the song, but the guy didn't even have a foot
pedal to keep the beat. In mainstream country songs at the time,
a foot pedal was rarely called for. We had no choice but to do
what we could and sing our hearts out. We got through it, but it
didn't sound much like the record. I don't mind saying it now—I
literally cried when we got off that stage. I thought that we had
blown our one big chance of turning the corner in our career.
What we performed didn't sound remotely like "My Home's in
Alabama" or "Tennessee River." We had been hamstrung by the
old Nashville ways.

Heartbroken, we dragged ourselves back to Myrtle Beach,
feeling totally defeated. The very next morning we got a call from
Nashville that three labels—RCA, Capitol, and Columbia—were
bidding for our services. Money aside, RCA sounded pretty good
to us. Three people there, it turned out, were instrumental in getting us noticed—the legendary Tony Brown, Sheila Shipley, and
Jerry Bradley. We were exposed to Joe Galante, later to become
the president of RCA in America, and they wanted to sign us and
rerelease *My Home's in Alabama* on RCA.

RCA had a sterling name in country music. It was the label
of Chet Atkins, among other greats, and they had been savvy
enough to sign Elvis Presley in 1955, after his early days with
Sun Records, for $35,000, an unheard of amount in those days.

RCA, originally the Victor Talking Machine Company, later RCA Victor, was the company that had sent a man named Ralph Peer to Bristol, Tennessee, in 1927 to record an obscure country group from the hills of Virginia called the Carter Family and a singing brakeman and yodeler named Jimmie Rogers, a seminal event in the history of recorded country music.

The old Nashville players at the New Faces gig didn't get what we were up to, and some of the people at RCA were a little baffled as well. When it came time to release "Tennessee River" as a single, they made us water it down a bit and drop the second verse to make it more palatable for country radio. It was a compromise I didn't want to make, but they held all the cards. When you hear the song in concert, you'll always hear the arrangement we created, including that second verse.

With *My Home's in Alabama* already making some waves and the corporate machine of RCA on our side, we were right at the starting gate, if not a little bit down the track. The single of "Tennessee River," our first megahit, was released in early 1980, following our signing with RCA a few months before. We played our last regular show at the Bowery on July 12, 1980. We'd come back a thousand more times to Myrtle over the next twenty-five years to see our fans and play on our home field, so to speak, and we later built the Alabama Theatre on Kings Highway there to cement the connection. But our seven-year apprenticeship with Bouncing Betty and playing covers at the Bowery was at an end. We were headed on down the line.

Unfortunately, in the worst kind of irony humanly possible, an event happened that would not only color the early years of Alabama, but also color the rest of my life.

> *I drove the van back to Alabama*
> *To find my mama alone*
> *She said, "Son, he's run a good race.*
> *And he's in a good place.*
> *Yea, a good place now."*
> "Good" by Randy Owen

CHAPTER 5

# G.Y.

*My dad was a big man with a will that was tough*
*He was at his best when the going got rough*
*He made a living for the family and never had to cheat*
*To keep food on the table and shoes on our feet*

"FOOD ON THE TABLE" BY RANDY OWEN

The year 1980 was shaping up to be big. My baby sister, Rachel, was about to graduate from high school and was planning a big wedding for April when she would marry Ricky Carroll, a man from the Sand Mountain area of Alabama. We were fixing to sign a record contract with RCA; our single, "My Home's in Alabama," was getting a load of airplay and moving up the record charts. I had a great wife who had stood by me during the uncertain years of the late '70s and a beautiful three-year-old daughter, Alison, who gave me all the more reason to get back home every chance I could. The general plan in the back of my brain—make it in the music business, raise a great family, make my daddy proud—was definitely taking shape, almost miraculously. I could feel God's hand directing me down the exact right path.

Alabama had just finished up a big event in Nashville in April, and we were about to head off for what would be our final summer at the Bowery in Myrtle Beach. It was a perfect time to get home for a day or two before we headed east. Kelly and I flew in, and Mama and Daddy picked us up at the Gadsden, Alabama, airport. Mama was driving our old Chevy van, as usual, as we rode back to Fort Payne. I told Daddy all about what was going on with the band. I said, "Daddy, I feel that things are fixing to happen; in fact, some good things already are happening." And I remember him saying, "Well, son, it's about time. You've worked awfully hard. You deserve some success."

That night Kelly and I visited with my grandparents, and while we were at their home, Daddy apparently had some kind of spell and didn't feel too good. When we got back home, he was lying on the couch and looking a little peaked. At that point I didn't know much about the history of his health, certainly not the recent history of other such episodes. I hadn't been around all that much since I first took off for college and then joined Teddy and Jeff in Myrtle Beach to plant the seeds of Alabama. Mama never told me that he had had these spells before when I wasn't there. Neither of them thought much about them, I guess. He'd be out working somewhere, start to feel bad, come home and rest a while, and then feel fine again. It was part of their general outlook, honed by years of poverty and tough times, not to complain or overreact to passing health concerns. He had never complained about his health when I was around between gigs, and he wasn't complaining now. He figured it was just part of getting old.

He also wasn't interested in getting checked out, before or now. Kelly, for one, was a little baffled that he didn't go to a doctor, but he figured that these little episodes that came and went were simply something he should endure, with God's help. My parents weren't Christian Scientists—they weren't opposed to doctors—they just saw such visits as an unnecessary expense, like going to a dentist every time you had a toothache.

That next day, as he seemed to be feeling better, I told him I had to go back to Myrtle Beach because we were about to start up again. I remember he was sitting in his bedroom, leaning on this chair, and he said, "Well, fine, go ahead, I'll be alright, don't worry." I said, "Daddy, I really don't want to leave you like this," but he wouldn't hear of it. My sister Rachel and her brand-new husband, Ricky, were around when this all happened, and they didn't seem that concerned either. As usual, we all took our cues from Daddy. He was not about to let me interrupt what looked like a rising music career because of a few temporary chest pains.

Plus, he was only fifty-nine. In fact, his fifty-ninth birthday had been two weeks before our visit. He was by all accounts still young and vigorous.

Kelly and I said our goodbyes and drove to Myrtle Beach in my yellow-and-black Camaro, the car we had dated in and that I still have out back. We were living in a trailer in Myrtle at the time, and so I dropped Kelly and baby Alison off at the trailer and went on down to the Bowery. That's when they told me the police were looking for me. Something had happened back home.

This was long before cell phones, so I went back, picked Kelly and Alison up, and found a pay-phone booth to call home. My sister Reba answered the phone and told me the awful news: our daddy had just died. He'd had a massive heart attack and died quickly. We'd only been gone from the farm for about nine or ten hours. In the interim he had died.

I can still visualize that moment. The weather was terrible. It was raining hard, and I remember the rain blowing on the side of the phone booth. I walked out into the rain to tell Kelly the news—and cry.

> *I broke down in that phone booth,*
> *talking to my family,*
> *My heart was soaking wet, and*
> *all I could do was cry.*
> *There's a lot to say in good-bye.*
> "THERE'S A LOT TO SAY IN GOOD-BYE"
> BY RANDY OWEN, RICHIE MCDONALD, AND GREG FOWLER

We tried to get a flight out of Myrtle Beach, but the next flight wasn't until late the next day. Leaving late that night in the pouring rain made no sense, plus I was too distraught to drive. The next morning we left the Camaro behind and got in the old blue beat-up band van, and with Teddy behind the wheel, the four of us—Teddy, Kelly, Alison, and I—drove the nine hours back to Fort Payne. When we came over the little hill to Mama's

Randy's parents, Martha and Gladstone Owen.

Randy in a hand-me-down toy car at their first house on Baugh Road on Grandpa Ernest Owen's place. This is where Gladstone and Martha lived when they first married. The toy truck was left by J.C. and Roger Hope, Randy's cousins, when they moved to Hawaii.

Randy with sisters Reba and Rachel. Randy holding a Supro guitar at the McMichen Place.

Randy at Chief's in Greenville, South Carolina, with the "music man" guitar played on "My Home's in Alabama," "Tennessee River," "Why, Lady, Why," "Mountain Music," and others.

Randy at the Bowery in Myrtle Beach, South Carolina, with "Bouncing Betty," the world's largest go-go dancer.

**THE ALABAMA BAND**

MYRTLE BEACH, S.C.   803-238-0573 or 803-448-4900

**WILDCOUNTRY, INC.**

P.O. BOX 529
FORT PAYNE, ALABAMA 35967
205-845-5087   205-845-4654

**MAYPOP MUSIC**
BMI
DIVISION OF
WILDCOUNTRY, INC.

Hi Terry,

My name is Randy Owen, member of the group "Alabama Band." Our group has released a new single, "I Wanna Come Over."

I'd like to thank you for finding the time to listen to the record and for playing it. Your help is greatly appreciated.

The group is currently working in Myrtle Beach, S.C., for the Summer. If you would like any information on the group, please write or call, at the address below, before Sept. 29.

Many Thanks!

Randy
"Alabama"

Randy Owen
Lot 2 Block 8
Scorpio Lane
Crystal Lakes Tr. Pk.
Myrtle Beach, S.C.
29577

(803) 238-0573

One of the handwritten letters that Randy and Kelly sent to radio stations.

Randy and Kelly Owen at Sesquicentennial State Park in Columbia, South Carolina.

Randy in Myrtle Beach, South Carolina, with Alison, while living in Benton's Trailer Park, where the song "My Home's in Alabama" was written.

Randy with Heath in 1983 signing autographs.

Randy's two oldest children, Alison and Heath.

The early years.

Randy, Alison, and Heath at the 1988 Alabama State Junior Heifer and Steer Show with their champion bull.

Randy and Grandma Teague.

Randy with his mother.

Greg Fowler, Kelly, Randy, and Dale Morris.

Randy at June Jam.

Randy in his 1972 Chevrolet Camero.

Randy, Heath, and Merle Haggard.

Randy, Kelly, and Dale Earnhardt, with Steve Boland, Heath Owen, and Jeff Rucks in the background.

Randy onstage at
June Jam, 1994.
© *Sheila Dykes*

Edna Hill United Methodist Church. This is where Randy's Paw Paw
Teague married his grandmother.

Randy performing the song "Angels Among Us."

The Owen family: (*left to right*) Kelly, Randa (*seated*), Randy, Alison, and Heath.

Randy and Hamlet 2 behind a Chevy pickup given to Randy by friend Leo Corley. The truck was operated on the historic R.W. Jones Hereford Ranch in Leslie, Georgia.

Randy, Kelly, Randa, and crew with Randa's Grand Champion Hereford Female at the 2008 Junior National Hereford Expo in Kansas City, Missouri. That fall Randa headed off to Auburn University and became a pre-veterinarian major.

Randy with kids at St. Jude.

house, I saw an ocean of cars. In fact, as far as you could see, up and down the road that led to her house, there were parked cars. There were also cars in the front yard and around the house. All the way from Myrtle, I kept hoping that when I got home, it wouldn't be true, that my daddy had somehow snapped back to life. When I saw all those cars, I knew it was true. Walking into that house was probably one of the hardest things I ever had to do. It was just awful.

When we entered, we saw the family and a room full of friends gathered around an open casket with my daddy lying in it. It was part of my parents' beliefs that you bring the body of the deceased home and not take him or her to a funeral home. Kelly had only seen this happen once before, with the death of one of her great-great-grandmothers in Anderson, South Carolina. This time, Kelly just backed away and watched our family go through the greatest suffering we had ever experienced together.

We buried Daddy next to his parents at the cemetery in Adamsburg only a few miles from his house. We pass it every time we take that route into Fort Payne. Daddy used to love to collect laurel flowers when we'd be out walking in the canyon and bring them home to Mama. So now, whenever the laurel blooms in the spring, Kelly will make a point of gathering some and placing them on his grave. It's a ritual we rarely let pass, no matter how busy we are.

I go down to the gravesite every chance I can, and it's never far away in my thoughts. I'm liable to tell Kelly, "You know, I stopped by Daddy's grave today on the way back from town." I usually think of it on my grandparents' anniversary or Father's Day or Daddy's birthday. The day of his passing is always a day of remembrance for me. I often retreat from the family and just keep to myself. Even now, twenty-eight years later, I tend to be pretty moody and testy on that day. I try to apologize to others when I act that way, but I don't apologize to myself. It's just a tough day, period. Despite all the good things that happen in this life, there are some wounds, I guess, that never quite heal, no matter how much time has elapsed.

Whenever I pull up to my parents' house to visit Mama, I can still see my dad, in my mind's eye, coming out of the barn or getting off his tractor in a nearby field. In some ways, it's comforting, knowing there is a certain continuity between his life and my own. In other ways, it's painful. It's a painful reminder of what wasn't to be.

Every time I sing the words to a largely autobiographical song like "Tennessee River," I see him again. Beginning when I was about three or four, Daddy used to drive me over to Scottsboro, Alabama, about thirty miles from home, every first Monday for a big open sale called First Monday. They sold and swapped everything—dogs, cows, cats, goats, sheep, hunting knives—you name it. People would come from all over, and even area politicians would show up at First Monday to press the flesh. For a country kid like me, it was like going to Lake Winnepesaukah for a day.

Coming off of Sand Mountain near Scottsboro, you could see the majestic Tennessee River flowing by. That's where the song of the same name, "Tennessee River," came from—taking in that view on the way to First Monday, along with another beautiful view when Daddy would take me along to Chattanooga to the auction barns. It was a very happy time in my life, and when I'm singing the song onstage, Daddy is sitting in the car seat right next to me. He is built right into that song.

My grief for my father runs deep, I think, because of the abrupt way he died at such an early age and at that particular time in my life. More than just a loving and caring father, he was my greatest supporter, especially when it came to music. He's the one who gave me the courage and confidence to do something like I set out to do. It was so crushing that he died before I got the break that would have brought him such joy and satisfaction.

My sister Reba tries to comfort me by telling me that we don't understand the reason why Daddy, a man who never hurt anyone and was such a great spirit, had to die, because we are not supposed to understand. That's where your faith comes in, she reminds me. You just have to live on faith that God knows what He's doing and that Daddy's death was part of God's plan, a plan that we are not privy to. Daddy, says Reba, is now in a better place and is present in all of our lives. The Bible says that God sends a ministry of angels to watch over us, and now Daddy is part of that ministry.

I understand Reba's message, but I felt utterly defeated when Daddy died, and I had no desire to rush back to work to chase the Alabama dream. It now seemed trivial and meaningless. Signing a big record contract, having a hit song on the radio, playing before a big crowd, being on TV—if I couldn't share this with Daddy, it seemed all that less important. It might be hard for other people to understand this bond and how it colored every aspect of my life, especially in this day and age when fathers, through divorce, personal ambition, or neglect, are often absent from a lot of kids' lives. Maybe I'm a throwback to an age when sons yearned to emulate their fathers and consider their father's approval to be a high mark of personal achievement. Throwback or not, that's how I felt then, and still do.

So I entered a very tough emotional period I guess you'd call "life after Daddy." I was used to his calling me at 7:30 in the morning, a time when he was headed out to trade cattle or buy fertilizer and a time I was usually just getting to sleep after playing music until 2:00 a.m. and then fooling around with my friends. "You're not asleep, are you?" he invariably asked.

But now that he was gone, the funeral was over, and all the relatives went back home, the music was again front and center. Everyone else connected to Alabama felt my sorrow, but they also knew our professional time was right now. I was in this totally dejected mood while dealing with all the pressures of people calling and telling me that now was the time to do this, go here, write this, call this radio station—that is, all the things you do to get a music group off the ground. Before long I found myself back on-stage, singing "My Home's in Alabama" or "Tennessee River," but now I was trying to keep from breaking down while I was singing the words. It was a weird juxtaposition of elation and grief, of feeling good to be performing and at the same time feeling bad to be performing, but I guess I was able to manage that emotional confusion because I was still young and had the psychic where-withal to handle the inevitable depression.

I had absolutely no time to grieve my father's passing, which meant the sadness got buried and became a permanent un-dercurrent in my life. I didn't have the luxury of taking off for six months and letting it sink in. I didn't have two days. I was back onstage, an audience full of brand-new Alabama fans was screaming and jumping up and down, and I felt like the loneliest guy on the planet.

In my mind, I had no choice about going back to work. It was clear this might be my only chance in life to make it in the music business and, in fact, fulfill my daddy's own ambition for me from the moment he sat me down to learn to play the guitar. It was my only chance to get away from the poverty that I had lived with growing up. Poverty doesn't make you a good person or a bad person, but it does make you a poor person, and those days of hand-me-down clothes and peas and okra for a month were still fresh in my mind. And growing up poor, as anyone who has been there will tell you, you never throw anything away, and that includes a career in country music.

Against my instinct to withdraw in the face of Daddy's death, I had to deliberately push myself in the other direction and remind myself over and over again to keep going. I had to will myself on-stage every night, no matter how I felt inside. This was my chance, as well as Teddy's and Jeff's chance, and I wasn't going to be the one to blow it. The upshot was that some of the saddest days of my life occurred before some of the biggest crowds we ever drew.

How fast were we moving at this tragic juncture in my personal life? By May 16, 1980, two weeks to the day my daddy had his heart attack, "Tennessee River" made it to No. 1, the first No. 1 song of forty-two for Alabama. On May 18, we had a concert in Columbus, Georgia, and then went on to perform at the Charlotte 600 NASCAR race in North Carolina on the 25th. In quick succession after that, we did a show in Greenville, South Carolina, an RCA showcase for executives, and a television appearance on the *Ralph Emery Show* in Nashville, followed by another in-studio radio appearance in St. Louis. And we were just warming up.

If you ask my sisters or mother why I continued on at this point, they'd probably sum it up as bullheaded stubbornness. Reba contends I got that trait from Mama, a woman never afraid to push herself until she got what she wanted. Reba also claims I have more faith than anybody she's ever known and a stronger belief that God's will *will* be done, and she also claims that people look at her like she's crazy when she says those things. I'm flattered that she thinks I have that much faith, whether she's crazy or not.

My faith was sorely tested in the aftermath of Daddy's death. I just didn't give a damn about life in general. If I was going to become an alcoholic or a drug addict, that would have been the perfect time to jump in feetfirst. Despite the assurances from my deeply faithful family that this was part of God's unknowable plan, I didn't get it. It seemed like a cruel joke to me. *Maybe,* I often thought, *I'm just being selfish.* Maybe I wanted Daddy to live so I could look good in his eyes. I know I feel bad that I never got to do anything for him, whether it was to take him on a long airplane flight, buy him a new tractor, or play beside him on the stage of the Grand Ole Opry. What I always longed to do was to give him $20,000 or whatever and say, "Here you go. Now go out and buy some registered cattle and do whatever you want to with them—breed them, sell them, or just put them out in a pasture and stare at them." If I could have done just that one thing, I could have lived a lot easier with his death.

On the gospel record that the Owen Family made, I sang solo on one song, as I said, the old Southern folk tune called "Silver Haired Daddy of Mine." Johnny Cash mentions in his autobiography that this was one of the songs he remembers from growing up in Arkansas. Daddy was still alive when I recorded that song, but it conveys a sense of regret, which I carried with me long after he died, a sadness summed up in lyrics like this:

> *If God would but grant me the power*
> *Just to turn back the pages of Time*
> *I'd give all I own if I could but atone*
> *To that silver haired Daddy of mine.*

I never really lost my faith in God, as I look back now, but I'll always feel a little bit swindled. And I'll never have an answer for the question, Why? That's probably what bothers me more than anything else. Why?

In the throes of all of this, there were loving people around to give me comfort and the strength to go on—Mama, Kelly, our three-year-old, Alison, and by the next year, 1981, our son, Heath. In the amazing way that kids sometimes see things, Heath would tell me as a toddler that he knew his grandpa. He'd never gotten to see him or be around him, but in his mind, he was sure he knew him. Alison did know him, and she and I talked about him a lot, so you can see where he got the idea. His grandpa was a living memory in our house. At one point I sat down with Alison and Heath, and we wrote a little song about Grandpa called "I Miss You, Papa. Everybody Misses You." Heath was all of eighteen months old at the time, but he sang along because he missed him too.

I also got solace and support from other people in the family, particularly my Mama's father, Paw Paw. One of the proudest moments of my life was when I was sitting in his house over on Mill's Creek in Cherokee County—he was in his mid to late eighties at the time—and he turned to me and said, "Randy, I'm proud of you, son." I was a little shocked because I didn't know he even knew what I did for a living, or cared about it. Apparently he sat around that old wood-burning stove of his and listened to the radio and was totally up-to-date. And I was deeply moved.

Following Daddy's death, after a period of mourning, Mama decided she wasn't ready to give up the Owen Family singing group. By this point, Reba's kids had grown up and could better take care of themselves, and Rachel's husband, Ricky, also supported the idea of keeping the family group going. So Reba joined Rachel and Mama as the core of the new Owen Family. Rachel was now a proficient bass player, Reba played tambourine, and Mama remained on the piano. Ricky now drove the old van when they made their short jaunts back and forth to local churches and served as their all-around roadie and stage technician. Rachel had a daughter, Mary, who learned to play the drums at a very young age and by all accounts turned into a star performer. In essence, Mama found a way of maintaining the kind of life she had always enjoyed. She worked around the farmhouse, kept working sewing toes down at the sock factory, and played gospel music with her two daughters while her "wayward" son was off making a name for himself.

All during the rise of Alabama in the 1980s, the Owen Family continued to play small country churches and perform at sing-ins all in that 75- to 100-mile radius of DeKalb County. But as time went on, it became harder and harder to get the group together. Mama was getting older, and both Reba and Rachel had growing kids to take care of. Also, Reba and her husband, Verlon, became an integral part of the Alabama road show, handling our ever-burgeoning merchandise concession when we were on tour.

With Daddy gone, Mama's attitude toward the music I was making became the dominant attitude in the family. She didn't really approve of it and offered no support at all. It's pretty un-derstandable, looking back on it. I was writing and performing secular popular music, music about romantic love and having a rowdy good time, not music tied to the church or the Christian faith. I was gone for long stretches from my wife and children and spent most evenings in bars and honky-tonks where, in her mind, all manner of sinful activity was taking place. I was pursu-ing a life, or at least associating with people pursuing a life, that was a long way from her definition of "clean" and "upright." Her faith was not the take-it-or-leave-it variety. There was bound to be some tension.

Because she was at home in Fort Payne much more than I was in those days, Kelly felt that tension and that quiet disregard for my music much more than I did. She had known my dad for five years and knew that his open-mindedness and enthusiasm was an important counterbalance to the feelings of others, but he was gone, and she felt she was without many allies in this regard. She recalls, "It wasn't real pleasant having to deal day to day with the nonsupport of his family. It was hard, really hard, for me to know how hard he was working and what a good person he was, and not be able to persuade them that just because he sang a certain kind of music didn't mean he was a different kind of person. They didn't look at it that way, and on many occasions, I had to bite my tongue and let their criticisms go right by me."

I love my mama dearly, then and now, and I love and respect the music and the gospel tradition she taught me as a child, but I had to forge my own path, along with Teddy and Jeff, and that path was secular country music. Despite the family's objections, I never gave any serious consideration to stopping our playing in Myrtle Beach and beyond, coming home, getting a job locally, and living "right." My definition of right was exactly what I was doing, and I had the support of my wife and closest friends in doing it. Our songs weren't salacious or rebellious or disrespectful of Christian life. But they were secular, not religious, and they were played in nightclubs and dance halls, not churches. Mama and I just had a difference of opinion and outlook that couldn't be easily resolved.

Kelly and I have often talked about how leaving Fort Payne and going to Myrtle Beach was one of the most important steps I ever took. It allowed me to see what I was really capable of as a singer-songwriter, both personally and in terms of the commercial music business. It was a clear choice all three of us in Alabama made early on. Our strong and abiding affection for the Carolinas grows out of the fact that it was one of the few places we could have gone to establish our craft and survive. Fort Payne and DeKalb County at the time were dry, meaning no alcohol could be sold or served. Even today, there are twenty-six counties in Alabama that are either totally dry or have "wet" cities. DeKalb now has a wet city, Fort Payne. Back then, though, there were not only no bars around there where we could perform; there were no bars, period.

A second reason why leaving Fort Payne was such a life changer for me is because in South Carolina I met and married Kelly, a girl young in years but one who had lived all over the country, not to mention Europe, and whose vision of what was possible was just as grand as my own. I had to leave my home behind, at least for a while, in order to attain the life I wanted and return as myself.

Mama and I get along fine, now—we always loved each other, despite our differences—and now I'm back home, more or less settled down, and even turning out a couple of very satisfying inspirational albums of late. I didn't become the wayward prodigal son after all. I didn't stray that far from the straight and narrow, at least in the way I define those terms. I just took a really long detour.

The death of my daddy certainly changed me and in some ways tempered all the success that was to follow. Dale Morris contends that the loneliness and sorrow I experienced in the wake of his passing altered the way I sang. He claims that it added a measure of soulfulness and longing to my voice that probably wasn't there before. I'm not arrogant enough to make pronouncements about the level of my singing or how other people should feel about it, but I do know that every time I sing "Ole Baugh Road" or any other song that evokes my childhood, I'm thinking about my dad and I am feeling his absence in my life. If that comes through in my voice, then I am doubly blessed that I had him as a father and that he still lives on in those notes.

With Daddy buried, we went back to work, and within a year of his passing, everything had changed—radically. If that day in May of 1980 was a date filled with sorrow and regret, many other memorable dates soon came to pass to help mitigate the sadness. One of the most important of those dates was June 12, 1981. Kelly was pregnant with Heath, and I had to be in Nashville for a whole week for a set of appointments with RCA. I told Kelly that whatever she did, she could not have that baby until after I got back on Friday night to witness the birth. Well, she didn't listen to me, or maybe it was the baby who didn't listen. Around 2:00 a.m. that Friday morning her water broke, and within two and a half hours, that boy was born. There was no way in hell I could have made it back. It was like my mama sitting in the car cooling her heels while we got married in front of Judge Gray—it all happened too fast.

Kelly called me with the exciting news, and a couple of hours later, Alabama walked onstage in Nashville to receive our very first gold album from RCA for the rerelease of *My Home's in Alabama*. A few years earlier, Alison had been born on my exact date of birth, and now Heath came along on the same day Alabama got its first major recognition.

As days go, that was a pretty damn good one. The Alabama train had clearly left the station, and I was about to spend the next two decades trying to catch up with it.

# CHAPTER 6

# ALABAMA ON FIRE

*I was July hot and 30*
*Some years down the line*
*When the boys touched the nation*
*unaware at the time*
*I got to go to Texas*
*California, New York too*
*A farm boy who is thankful*
*To be standing in his shoes*

"TAR TOP" BY RANDY OWEN

Dale Morris was the right man at the right time to take over the management of Alabama and lead us to a level of success and accomplishment we had never dreamed of. Dale was born in Inman, South Carolina, and originally came to Nashville to be a songwriter. He got a few original songs out there, my favorite being "Don't Monkey with Another Monkey's Monkey," recorded by Johnny Paycheck, the man who brought you "Take This Job and Shove It." Dale eventually moved into artist management, and when Alabama came along, he had two main clients. One was Billy "Crash" Craddock, a popular country star at the time who was once given the title Mr. Country Rock because of his energetic, up-tempo music. His other big client was Terri Gibbs, blind from birth, who had a huge hit in 1981 with a tune called "Somebody's Knockin'." When we arrived in town for good, Dale was a seasoned Nashville veteran with a sterling reputation for honesty and fairness. He was the steady hand and creative vision-ary we needed.

As Dale will tell you, country shows of any size were pretty hard to book back in those days, especially outside of the South. Almost anyone who loved country music would buy a ticket to see Conway Twitty, Loretta Lynn, or other legends of the era like Merle Haggard, Buck Owens, or Johnny Cash. Johnny Cash, backed by June Carter and the legendary Carter Family, could play big halls like Cobo Hall in Detroit, but he was a rarity. Un-fortunately, we had to learn this lesson the hard way.

One of the first dates we did under Dale and Barbara's tute-lage was somewhere in Ohio. Dale remembers this story well. It was a very bleak night, attendance-wise. Dale and Keith Fowler stood out in the lobby that night trying to sell a ticket to anyone who walked by. A person would stroll in, and Keith would whis-per to Dale, "Hey, I think she might buy one. Maybe." It was bad. As Dale would later put it, "we got our butts handed to us that night."

By the time ticket sales were added up, we had lost about $7,000 for the evening. Actually, the promoter had lost $7,000, and we had lost whatever part of the take that was contractually due us. Under the circumstances, that was zero. Dale was the one who had to come backstage and give us the bad news. When he said, "Boys, I hate to tell you this, but tonight we lost seven thousand dollars," Teddy immediately replied, "How are we going to pay back seven thousand dollars? We don't have seven thousand dollars just sitting around!" Dale had to explain that it didn't work that way. The promoter ate the seven grand; it was his loss, not ours. We were very relieved. Dale claims we were just as happy to hear that we didn't *owe* money for playing a show as we would have been if we'd just pocketed ten grand.

We were, in a word, naive. We needed all the help we could get.

We went back down South where we knew we could find a more receptive atmosphere. Because of our long stint at Myrtle Beach, we had enough people who knew us and would plop down some money to see us at a small club venue. As Barbara remembers—and she booked every last gig—we set out to play wherever possible in 1981 and ended up doing 280 dates. We started out working small clubs with capacities of maybe a few hundred if you squeezed everyone in, and we figured we were doing pretty well. We were making a good living, and that was saying a lot back then. Barbara already had the summer schedule pretty well booked up, because you tended to book summer, the busiest season for traveling musicians, a few months in advance.

It was time now to leave behind the familiar South-only strategy, and when we came out to the rest of America, to quote Dale, "it was like a flight lifting off going straight to the moon."

The album *My Home's in Alabama* was certified gold by June, and well before that we'd had three No. 1 country singles— "Tennessee River" in May of 1980, as mentioned, plus "Why, Lady, Why" in September of 1980, and "Old Flame" in January of 1981. At the time all of this was unfolding, we were making maybe $4,000 or $5,000 a concert. Then the calls started coming in to Barbara that someone wanted us on one of our off days and would pay $25,000. No way were we going to pass that up, no matter how many performances we had to do in a row. All of a sudden we were staying out for thirty or more days at a time. And we rarely missed a show. It was inconceivable to us to miss a show, no matter what the fee. We might have been naive, but we understood hard work and weren't a bit afraid of it. This was our time. We would have plenty of time to sleep later on.

Our mode of transportation in those days was a used, twenty-year-old Marshall Tucker Band touring bus with a bobtailed trailer behind. We called it the Old Blue Goose. One time we were driving down the road and people were looking at us and honking and we couldn't exactly figure out why. When we stopped, we realized that some side covering had come off the bus to reveal the name Marshall Tucker. Hell, we were famous, or at least our bus was.

We crammed everything into that trashy old vehicle, including ourselves and eight to ten crew guys. Barbara often came with us too, and she remembers the smell. It was horrible.

Riding across the country in the Old Blue Goose, there was no room for a costume department. We'd pull into a place like Des Moines for a concert, and if I needed a clean shirt to wear onstage, I'd grab something that would invariably have the word "Iowa" on the front and throw it on. The hometown crowd loved it, I loved it, and not one person said, "Why aren't you wearing a purple velour leisure suit?"

It got to the point that someone would give me a local shirt at every single stop, and sometimes dozens of them. I'd start with one given to me backstage, then grab one tossed to me by a fan during the show, take the sweaty one off, throw it out to the crowd, put on the new one, and keep playing. I wouldn't even look to see what the next shirt said. I learned to stop that after I looked down one night and saw a shirt with a mouse on the front, purring, "Here, kitty, kitty, kitty." If you have a picture of me in that shirt, do me a favor and burn it.

I think the best description of an Alabama show from those early days comes from Marc Oswald, a concert promoter who later came to Nashville, became a top manager, and ended up managing or co-managing some major names like Gretchen Wilson, Big and Rich, and . . . me. Marc remembers the first time he saw Alabama in concert. It was April 1981, and Marc and his brother, Greg, now a top William Morris agent, were promoting concerts in San Diego part-time while working day jobs as paramedics. The first national act they booked was Alabama. The show, in San Diego, happened the same week that "Feels So Right," the same song I sang to Kelly when I was first courting her at her home in Columbia, South Carolina, became Alabama's fourth No. 1 single.

In 1981, as I said, country acts by and large had a static stage presence. Whether the Statler Brothers or Charlie Pride, they came onstage, backed by their road band, stood in front of microphones, and sang. People came to hear the songs and see their musical idols in person and weren't expecting a spectacular stage show with a lot of lights and noise. Everybody, onstage and off, tapped their toes and had a good time. It was leisurely and sedate, and the music always satisfied.

We came onstage like a house afire. In the same frame of mind as in our dues-paying days at the Bowery, we were there to show the audience a good time and to have a good time ourselves. We didn't take our cues from the smooth, laid-back country-show tradition. We learned our stage chops in a rock-'n'-roll bar. We were there to raise the roof.

Here's Marc's description of that show in San Diego: "They were all over the stage like a rock act. They were flying everywhere. And they incited a sort of positive riot in the audience. They were playing country music, for sure, but they were playing it with all the intensity and energy you'd get if you'd paid to see Tom Petty or Bon Jovi. It was wild and it was loud. They were up there jumping around, and they were playing their own instruments, like any other rock band. They weren't up there to sing their hits. They were there to engage the audience, interact with them, wake them up. It was so novel in country music, it felt like a revolution. It was insane, insane energy."

The stage production in those days wasn't big. It was just the four of us out there. Because we were so versatile, we could play every instrument we needed, from guitar to fiddle. We were self-contained and tight. That all added to the energy level. And we looked like the guys next door. We looked like we'd just walked out of a locker room, wearing our team football jerseys. We always wore everyday pants, and our footgear varied from python boots to tennis shoes to occasionally flip-flops. Our hair was unruly, and we rarely wore hats, cowboy or otherwise. It all said, "Relax, let loose, have a good time. God knows, we plan to."

Barbara remembers one time in 1980 when we had been booked into a state fair for about our going rate of five grand. The promoter was one of our favorites, named George Moffitt, who was constantly smoking a cigar and had been around the country scene for a long time. He knew the flowery dresses and glittery suits and pompadour hairstyles that country fans were used to. Just before the show, he went up to Dale and said, "You know, Dale, we got about five minutes before they go on—I think the boys ought to get dressed now." Dale said, "Well, George, they are dressed." George said, "You're s**tin' me! No one dresses like that!" No one, I guess, but us.

A booking sheet is a standard music-business form that bookers like Barbara use to keep track of a performer's schedule. If you looked at the booking sheet for Alabama from 1981, around the same time as that concert in San Diego, you'd see how crazy things were. We were out West at the time, but we could have been in any part of the country. Here's a brief example of what I'm talking about:

Fri, March 6: Modesto, CA

Sat, March 7: Imperial, CA

Sun, March 8: Santa Barbara, CA

Mon, March 9: Bakersfield, CA

Tues, March 10: Imperial Beach, CA

Wed, March 11: Phoenix, AZ

Thurs, March 12: *Opryland* TV show, CBS, LA

Sat, March 14: CLUB TO COME, LA

Sun, March 15: San Carlos, CA

Tues, March 17: *Solid Gold* TV show, LA

Wed, March 18: Las Vegas, two nights

Fri, March 20: Salt Lake City, UT

We didn't have a real solid overview of what we were doing. We were just doing it. It was not like we all sat down one Sunday afternoon and said, "Okay, we'll play like a rock band, with fiddles and other country instruments, of course, and we'll dress like we always dress, and we'll jump around onstage and make people forget what they thought a country act should be and just have a good time." None of these things were preplanned. It just evolved out of the music we liked and the way we liked to play it. We weren't smart enough to prepackage ourselves. We were too busy trying to get to the next gig.

We had no idea what the audience was getting out of all this except for the ton of fan mail we were starting to receive and the

brief nightly interchange with fans when we were signing autographs. One person I knew who could give me a pretty good idea
of a fan's point of view was Sue Leonard, a wonderful woman
who has worked with Dale and Barbara since before Alabama
entered their lives. Sue was, and is, a trusted business associate,
but she was also a fan. She, like many others, didn't really care for
country music until she started listening to Alabama.

"These guys came along, and all of a sudden I'm going, 'I love
country music!' They were like the boys next door. They seemed
humble and easy to get to know. And even though it was country,
the music made you feel so good you thought you were listening
to rock-'n'-roll. I really and truly feel that Alabama did for country what the Beatles did for rock-'n'-roll. They were fresh and
exciting. They didn't seem like the type to drink or do drugs. You
weren't afraid of letting your kids go see them. You wanted to be
around them. You could identify with both them and what they
sang about. They were just everyday, average, incredible stars."

Asked about her favorite song, Sue replied, "Oh, 'Feels So
Right.' I just knew Randy was singing it for me. But don't tell Kelly."

If someone back then had compared us to the Beatles, I
would have laughed out loud, and looking back, it's still a major,
major stretch. But we did strike a different chord in country
music, I think it's fair to say, and early on we had some industry
fans who proved to be enormously helpful in getting our music
heard. Very high on the list was Dick Clark.

Dick Clark booked us for the first time on *American Bandstand*, the most popular TV music show at the time, on October 4,

1980. *American Bandstand* was a pop music show for teenagers. It featured every genre of American popular music that Dick Clark thought his teen audience would like. We appeared on the show that also featured Tanya Tucker. President Jimmy Carter had declared that week Country Music Week, so Dick booked a whole week of crossover country acts.

Dick had been featuring country stars on *American Bandstand* since the 1950s. The only act who ever turned him down, he says, was Porter Wagoner. Porter was booked, but when he got to Philadelphia for the taping, they told him they only paid scale, so he left. By the time we were asked to do *Bandstand,* we would have paid Dick to let us play. It was exposure that money couldn't buy.

Dick seemed to understand what we were about from the very beginning and knew that our music had an appeal far beyond the then-existing boundaries of the country genre. "They were one of the first groups to blend rock and country music," he later said. "They had broad appeal. Plus, they were true to their music and devoted to their fans. They kept the ship all together and treated it like a business, in addition to a career in music. They had it all."

Our relationship and friendship with Dick stretched from that day in 1980 all the way through the 1980s and '90s to today. Through the great help of Dick, Gene Weed, Bill Boyd, and others in his operation, we appeared on many of his shows, including the *Academy of Country Music Awards, Dick Clark's New Year's Rockin' Eve,* and others, and he even graced us with his presence at one of our June Jam festivals in Fort Payne in 1986. And Dick is quick to point to our success in winning the American Music Award, an award ceremony he himself created. All told, we ended up being honored with twenty-three American Music Awards, the most in the history of the award, even ahead of legendary winners like Whitney Houston and Michael Jackson. In myriad ways, Dick Clark opened the door to our exposure to millions of fans who had never heard of Hank Williams or George Jones.

We were so fortunate to arrive as a group when we did. For whatever reason, our timing was just right. As I have often said about the era of music we walked into: "Thank God for disco."

Disco music had dominated much of the popular music business in the 1970s. There were many other things going on in music, from the Eagles to Willie and Waylon and the Outlaw movement in country to Bruce Springsteen's *Born to Run* and the Moody Blues. But disco was huge for millions of radio listeners, and when we arrived, it was waning, and a lot of kids were looking for some alternative. We didn't fit the standard mode of a live-fast, die-young rock-'n'-roll group, we weren't traditional country, and we sure weren't disco. Disco was dance music, with lyrics that were generally either self-referencing—"Let's dance tonight!"—or inane or both. We entered the fray with story songs. It's a long way from "Get Down Tonight" to "Tennessee River." And a lot of music fans were ready for that change.

It didn't take long for us to realize we could do shows and sell tickets on our own, without being part of a multiact lineup. We only did about ten shows as an opening act. We quickly built to the point where we were our own opening act and closing act. Initially, we worked with all the big regional promoters who would pay us a flat fee and reserve most of the profit, if there was a profit, for themselves. But soon you could no longer "buy" Alabama, that is, negotiate a fee for our services. We joined forces with our own built-in promoter, Keith Fowler, who made all the appearance arrangements for the group. If you wanted Alabama at your local arena or civic center, you had to go to Keith to make the deal. Soon we were competing with the biggest music promoters in the business for bookings. We did it all ourselves—booking, ticket sales, merchandise sales, the whole show. I personally didn't know how other bands did it, but I knew that's how we did it, and Dale, Barbara, and Keith oversaw everything. Soon we added our own music publishing company—called Maypop—to the mix. It gave us all the more creative and financial control of our lives. (The Maypop, in case you were wondering, is a flower–passion fruit indigenous to our corner of the world.)

We didn't play big stadiums in this superhot period because that wasn't much of an option in those days. We might play a stadium in conjunction with a football game, say, in Denver or Texas, but mostly we played arenas and a lot of state fairs. We also hit as many small towns as we could. We never hesitated to go anywhere we thought there was an audience who wanted to hear us.

As Dale has said, "In our business, you've got to make hay while the sun shines. And we continued to make that hay in the sunshine for almost thirty years."

The point when I personally began to understand that what we were doing was making bigger waves than I ever imagined came in West Palm, Florida, sometime in 1980. We were on tour at the time, doing mostly small clubs, but this was an arena situation. Backstage the noise we heard from out front sounded like a jet plane fixing to land. It was a constant roar. I remember being back there and asking, "Wow, who else is playing here tonight? They must be big. Listen to that."

Then we walked out onstage, and it was mayhem. The place was packed, and kids were screaming and yelling, throwing things, pitching underwear onstage, just completely going wild. The noise was overpowering. We didn't have a sound system that could possibly compete with that kind of crowd noise, but the crowd didn't seem to care. Even though we only had one certified hit at the time, "Tennessee River," they seemed to sing along to every song we played, and they were singing a hell of a lot louder than we were. It was crazy and a little disorienting, but it was fun.

That experience began to be repeated pretty much all the time. We would walk into a place like the Rupp Arena in Lexington, Kentucky, and it would be so loud and rambunctious we could barely hear ourselves sing and play. We were still only getting anywhere from $3,500 to $5,000 to perform, but we knew it was no longer about that particular payday. It was about the amazing energy and enthusiasm of the people who came to see us. And in those early days, we were as eager to play small-town venues of 2,500 people as we were to book the big-city ones with 25,000. It was a smart strategy—we went to where the fans were, and they appreciated it.

Greg Fowler joined us full-time as our publicist and all-around problem solver in 1981, and he remembers that transition from an Alabama performance to an Alabama event. Once we got to playing arenas, all we had to do was announce we were coming to your town to play, and the ticket rush was on. "I mean," Greg remembers, "word got out, and it was over. People would camp out to get tickets, and I don't mean camp out overnight. I mean camp out for days and days. They would hold their places in the ticket line with their chairs and blankets night and day, whether it was snowing or not. This was before the Internet or online buying. You had to physically go get a ticket. And they did."

Once inside, we tried to give them a show. When we arrived in San Diego for the show with Marc Oswald, we were all in that one smelly Marshall Tucker bus. Within a year or so, we'd pulled into Minneapolis or Gainesville with four or five tour buses and six or seven beautiful fly trucks full of equipment, all necessary for a tightly organized high-production-value stadium show.

Largely due to the influence and insight of Dale, we aspired to create a show that rivaled any major rock act at the time. I remember one time I went to a Bob Seger concert in Memphis to see his kind of stage production and how much it inspired me to be more creative in mounting our own show. Thanks to people like Ricky Farr, who brought in our high-powered light-and-sound tech, we ended up with some of the most innovative stage lighting for the period, moving lights that would spotlight each of us onstage as we took a solo. We had all kinds of stage rigging, from elevator lifts to big drop curtains, called Kabuki curtains, that we would emerge from behind. We finally found a sound system big enough to handle that kind of massive crowd environment. We'd turn it up loud, and the kids would want it louder. Some of the more traditional country fans who came out to see us probably had to adjust to the mayhem, but they kept coming. As Dale once said, "We'd put the sound on eleven even though it only went to ten."

As we ventured further and further away from our Southern base, we had to confront one sticky issue: the rebel flag. If you look at certain Alabama album covers, beginning with *My Home's in Alabama* in 1980, you'll see the Confederate flag somewhere in the picture. Early on we took our cues on this from the Alabama state flag, which is two thick red lines crisscrossing against a white backdrop. Call us naive, but where we came from in the backwoods of northern Alabama, that symbol was simply a matter of regional pride and identity and nothing else. We didn't use it as a signal about our feelings about black people or to make a political statement or anything, anymore than someone would wear an Oklahoma Sooners sweatshirt to piss off people in Texas. Before it became a controversy, we left any sign of the flag off all of our branding and stuck with our unique graphic of the word "Alabama."

We sure didn't want to limit our audience to people who were still fighting the Civil War. If our music wasn't traditional country, it wasn't traditional Southern, either, and certainly not in its appeal. We love living in the South, no doubt about it, but we came along when people outside of the South still saw the

South in stereotypical ways—to put it bluntly, ignorant, racist, backward—and we thought it was important to take our music elsewhere and maybe open a few eyes. I hope we did. All I can tell you is audiences loved us in the Midwest, among other regions, and they were probably people who had never picked a boll of cotton or eaten a piece of sweet-potato pie.

We got our knocks in the press that we were too country, not country enough, too slick, too pop, or too commercial for the cause of good music, but when we walked onstage, what we saw was a place packed to the walls with people going crazy and having the time of their lives, and they could pick up a reasonably priced T-shirt or hat on their way out. We were playing many of the same basketball-game-sized buildings, to many of the same people, as the biggest rock acts of the day—acts like Bob Seger, John Mellencamp, Alice Cooper, Styx—sometimes with two shows in one day. And we could fill those buildings as fast as anyone.

A whole army of people helped make those shows happen over the years, from Terry Cologne and his family, who were instrumental early on in the design and marketing of our merchandise, to all the wonderful promotional people at RCA. At one point we had one whole bus full of nothing but people involved in the merchandise end. And we had concert promoters like Bob Romeo and his dad handling events like rodeos and fairs, and others like George Moffitt, Barry Fey, and Jimmy Jaye who were vital in getting us into the right venues.

When we came to a new place to play, we had a system that ensured we'd be as accessible to both the media and the fans

as possible. Around 4:00 p.m. on a performance day, we'd hold
a press conference, and we'd all be there to answer any and all
questions and try not to show favoritism to any media outlet,
big or small. Then we'd have some pictures taken and sign some
autographs for special guests, like radio call-in winners, then we'd
do a sound check onstage, cool off a little, and then do the show.
After every show would be the big autograph session. We would
sign autographs after every single show, and we wouldn't leave
until the last person left. We'd be at, say, the Minnesota State Fair
or an arena in Richmond, Virginia, and people would be lined up
all the way around the venue or all the way down into the fourth
turn of a milelong raceway, and it could be cold or rainy, but we'd
happily stay out there and sign every poster, T-shirt, or back of
the program. Sometimes the road crew would have completely
torn down the stage set and packed it into the trucks, and we'd
still be smiling for pictures with the last bunch of fans. We might
start with a press conference at 4:00 in the afternoon and end
with one more autograph at 2:00 in the morning. To us, it was
just part of the show—meet the fans afterward.

But most people didn't come to a show mainly for the lights,
the sound, the autographs, or the T-shirts. They came for the
music.

Writing songs like "Face to Face" and "Lady Down in Love"
is both a matter of inspiration and craft. I was always very proud
about how we could craft a song in a way that made it both
memorable and exciting. When I started writing back in high
school, I really didn't know what I was doing, but I knew what I

liked. I liked songs with a unique, individual sound, a signature lick or phrase, or, to use the common musical language, a hook. This could be either a guitar or other instrumental hook or a lyrical one. A lot of the songs I loved as a kid, both country and rock, had that kind of sound in which the minute the song came on the radio, you knew what it was. For instance, a song I really liked while growing up was "Secret Agent Man," by Johnny Rivers. "There's a man who leads a life of danger . . ." If you know the song, the minute you even read the title, you start singing it in your head. It has that one-of-a-kind hook to it.

This is equally true with a country classic like Bobby Bare's "Detroit City," also known as "I Wanna Go Home." The minute you hear the phrase "I wanna go home," you're singing along. The lyric line is unforgettable, as is the recurring low guitar lick. The difference between this and "Secret Agent Man" is that the latter is a song about a make-believe spy "swingin' on the Riviera," and "Detroit City" is about a man stuck in a factory job who wants to go back home in the South. It's a real story.

Signature licks or hooks are hard to create and if you're lucky enough to find the right ones to fit a melody and lyric, that song can have a long, long life. Most of the big Alabama hits have a definable hook. Take "Tennessee River." As I mentioned earlier, the lyrics of this song refer to my own experience of seeing that river with my daddy on the way to Scottsboro, Alabama, every first Monday of the month. The lyrics generalize from that and talk about things we hope for in our lives—to relive the good times of growing up and settling down "where peace and love can still be found." Growing up in the 1960s and '70s, when wars raged and a president and other leaders were assassinated, peace and love were longed for by millions.

But, musically, the first thing you hear in "Tennessee River" is some eerie background sounds and a single guitar. It's a kind of futuristic-sounding rhythm guitar that to me sounds like you're going underwater and then back to the top again, like you were swimming in a river. When you hear that strangely melodic opening, you know the song that's coming. It sounds like a small thing, but successful three-minute popular songs are made up of many small things.

Then the song begins with its slightly up-tempo Southern-rock melody. You're singing along, hopefully enjoying the feeling of being in that peaceful country place, when all of a sudden, the tempo completely shifts, and you're tearing it up with a hell-raising bluegrass fiddle. It is almost two songs in feel, like you were lying by the river and suddenly decided to get up and dance and kick your heels. Now imagine hearing that song in an arena full of 18,000 rowdy fans. They are just waiting for that shift when Jeff kicks in with that fiddle and we blow the roof off of the house. When I wrote the song, I had Jeff's playing firmly in mind; in a sense, I was writing the song to build to his solo.

Other songs have other hooks and feature other aspects of Alabama's versatility, like adding a bass solo by Teddy to "My Home's in Alabama," but that sudden shift in tempo in many of our songs was entirely new to country music at the time. Guns N' Roses' "Paradise City" makes me think of this. Rock songs often altered rhythm and melody in the middle of a song, but to country-radio programmers, it sounded a little strange. Plus, we were mixing rock instruments with fiddles. This was a period when country music was increasingly pop oriented in its sound—the so-called country-pop movement—and we were told that country radio was trying its best to get rid of bluegrass. Bluegrass was old music and reminded people who didn't like it of hillbillies in overalls with chews of tobacco in their jaws and a car on blocks in the front yard. They didn't want to hear banjos, mandolins, and especially not fiddles. There were no fiddles in the music of Olivia Newton-John or Anne Murray. Fiddles were old school.

So we come along with a song that suddenly breaks into a pure bluegrass fiddle riff, not watered down with strings or overdubbing or any other softening effect. From the perspective of today, where the most popular country artists will proudly include anything from steel guitars to mandolins to stand-up basses and celebrate the whole history of country music in their songs—where Gretchen Wilson will proudly evoke the name of the great George Jones—it seems kind of silly that having a fiddle in the band caused any controversy. We got the song past the naysayers, even though they removed a verse to make it acceptable to radio, and by the time it hit No. 1, the controversy was over. And the audience never even knew there was a controversy.

We kept Jeff's fiddle at the heart of our music. When we released the song "If You're Gonna Play in Texas (You Gotta Have a Fiddle in the Band)," though we didn't write it ourselves, we certainly gave the fiddle its due. When it became our fourteenth straight No. 1 country song, I doubt if there was a person in the country-music business who was mumbling, "They might really make it if they'd just drop that damn fiddle from their sound."

Another signature song from the beginning was "Mountain Music," a pure Alabama song in every way. It took me three years to write it, and I wanted to get my own experience of growing up in the mountains in the lyrics. This came together in such very specific lines. Take, for instance, the stanza that begins "swim across the river, just to prove that I'm a man." When I was a kid, if you could make it across the Little River and back in one fell swoop, well, that was a big deal. It doesn't look that wide today, but back then it seemed like an Olympian challenge.

Another key lyric is "playing baseball with chert rocks, using sawmill slabs for bats." Chert rocks are a kind of hard gravel you find in the mountain ridges in this area. Since the soil here is very sandy, chert rocks are mixed into the surface of dirt roads and make the going a lot easier. During the rainy season, you don't end up in as many ditches as my granddad used to fifty years ago.

We loved to use those rocks as baseballs, since real baseballs were hard to come by, so I stuck that detail into the song. Not that everybody got what I was talking about. I remember one interview after the song came out where this woman asked how my mother liked that song. I said, "She likes it fine," and the interviewer replied, "Well, being such a Christian woman, I bet she especially likes the line about the 'church' rocks."

Chert rocks almost got me in a lot of trouble, or so I thought at the time. After Alabama hit the big time, we were invited to a very elegant dinner in New York with the president of RCA Records. As a butler served up the food, our host, the executive who basically controlled our commercial fortunes, asked me about the song "Mountain Music," especially the line about "chert rocks." I started to tell him the story of using them on the roads back home, and he stopped me and said, "Well, I don't know what you call them back there, but 'chert' is really not a word." He said this like he was 100 percent certain he was right. I said, "Well, sir, I think it is a word and I think it is spelled c-h-e-r-t." He then tells the butler to get a dictionary so he can look it up and prove his point.

I'm sitting there thinking, *What if it really isn't a word and the president of RCA thinks we're a bunch of idiots and kicks us off the label?* The butler brings back the dictionary and shows it to the man, and praise the Lord, there it is: "chert—a compact rock consisting essentially of microcrystalline quartz." I was right and he was wrong. And though I'm sure it had nothing to do with the chert controversy, eventually he left the company.

Anyway, after "Tennessee River," then "Why Lady Why," then "Old Flame," then "Feels So Right," then "Love in the First Degree," then "Mountain Music"—all No. 1 songs before the end of 1981—we focused on turning out a string of No. 1 hits for the next twenty-one songs. We were a hit machine. That was the whole goal. No. 2 or 3 wasn't good enough, or at least so we thought at the time. A good way to grasp our goal it is to compare us with NASCAR racers today. No one lines up at the starting line of the Daytona 500 to come in second. Every driver has only one thing on his mind—being the first guy to see the checkered flag. We were the same way. We knew we made music that an increasingly large audience responded to, and we were there to deliver that audience bona fide hits.

And, hey, getting those publishing royalty checks in the mail wasn't bad. I remember receiving my first royalty check like it was yesterday. We were still playing in Myrtle Beach, and I walked out to the mailbox one morning and saw an envelope clearly marked BMI, the performing-rights organization that distributes royalties to songwriters, long run by an incredible, loving woman named Frances Preston. Anyway, I saw that envelope, and my heart started pounding. *Oh, boy,* I thought, *this is royalty money!* I tore it open and saw two checks—one for $.25 and one for $.75. I was so proud. All I could think was that I had a dollar more than I had when I went to the mailbox. The checks got bigger, of course—in fact, an advance from Frances allowed us to build the house we live in today—but that first one will always stay with me.

As I said, from our earliest Bowery days we were an audience-oriented band, so we crafted our songs to appeal to two audiences—the radio audience and the live one. We'd record a song one way to make it radio-friendly, then open it up and provide a completely different experience onstage. That might mean segueing out of nowhere into a few bars of "Country Roads," if we were in West Virginia, or getting the audience involved in clapping, chanting, or singing all the lyrics themselves. The point was to say to every audience in every situation, "Hey, we're aware of you, we love you, and we appreciate that you're spending your money to be here because it means a lot to us and our families." That's a much different attitude than thinking you're doing the audience a favor by showing up and running through your radio hits, oblivious to what they are bringing to the party.

Responding to that audience, night after night, along with that NASCAR-driver obsession with winning every race, forced me to maintain a laserlike focus on what I was doing. This probably explains why I never got sidetracked by drugs or alcohol. There was plenty of dead time on the road—getting to a gig, waiting around for a gig to start, getting to the next gig—where I certainly had the time for some recreational imbibing. But I had to write another hit song or do another interview or make a friendly call to another radio station or—something I still do to this day—answer another fan letter. Maybe I was just lucky. Maybe it was because of my strict upbringing. Maybe I didn't want to blow it. Or maybe I just enjoyed feeling good and not hungover or wasted when it was time to hit that stage.

As we continued to turn out the original nonstop string of No. 1 songs, I almost felt guilty because we were writing most of them while all of the writers in Nashville were trying to get their songs to us to record. In one sense, it was an honor to have perhaps the best songwriting community in the world beating down your door with new songs because they thought you could make them a hit. On the other hand, you're faced with the pressure of publishing companies and record executives pushing you to record a song simply because they knew it could be a hit with your name on it. There's a line that's crossed when you end up releasing a song that's catchy and clever but has absolutely nothing to do with who you are, where you came from, or what you truly want to say. Soon you're putting commercial success over creativity, identity, and roots. And in doing so, you've watered down your music and made it less special.

I'm afraid, at least from my own perspective, that Alabama began to cross that line in pursuit of always being number one. It threw us, as a group, musically off kilter; it threw me, as a singer-songwriter, into a lot of second-guessing about what I was doing with my life.

There really isn't enough space in this book to talk about all the Alabama hits and misses, the ones I loved and the ones I didn't. That will have to wait for the more definitive Alabama book where we all can weigh in about our collective songbook. I can tell you this, though: every Alabama song I wrote or co-wrote was monumental in my life. Each one connects to me deeply, either because it is directly autobiographical, like "Tennessee River" or "Feels So Right," or because it comes from personal observation. "Lady Down on Love," one of my favorites to this day, is a song that carries a back story with it, a story I often relate in concert to the audience before I perform it. Here's that story, briefly.

In 1976, when we were still called Wildcountry, we were booked to play at a Red Carpet Inn in Bowling Green, Kentucky. Those were the days when we more or less did what the guy paying us told us to do. This guy, I remember, wanted us to wear matching leisure suits, a horrible experience, and he wanted us to go out and talk to the customers and find out what they'd like to hear. So I walked up to this table of young women and asked them what the big occasion was, and they pointed to one of their party and said, "We're here to celebrate her divorce." We all laughed about this common scenario, but then I spotted the new divorcée down at the other end of the table and noticed that she didn't seem too happy. I asked her about that, and she said, "I'm not happy. I'd really rather be at home, be with my husband, and still be in love."

This comment really stuck with me. Usually a woman in that situation would say that she was glad to get rid of the sucker and be "free" again, and all her friends would chime in about what a loser the guy really was. But not this woman. She gave me a surprisingly frank, heartfelt response. And the next words out of her mouth became the first line of the song I wrote about her. "You know," she said, "this is the first time I've been out on the town like this since I was eighteen years old." The song begins with:

> *It's her first night on the town since she was*
> *just eighteen, a lady down on*
> *Love and out of hope and dreams.*
> *The ties that once bound her now are broke away,*
> *and she's like a baby, just*
> *Learning how to play.*

I ran back to my motel room and wrote that song as fast as I could. I thought if I could just get it to Johnny Rodriquez, a huge star at the time, I would have a No. 1 country hit and be on my way as a songwriter. I even switched the lyrics of the last verse to tell this sad story from the man's point of view, with a guilty plea that "I gave in to lust, and she just couldn't live with a man she couldn't trust."

It didn't work out with Johnny Rodriquez, I'm happy to report, and we recorded it for the first time soon after for the Wildcountry album *Deuces Wild* in 1977. Later we rerecorded it as Alabama, and I've always felt that I finally got to do it exactly the way I wanted—the exact right guitar-solo intro, the exact right string arrangement by Kristin Wilkinson, the exact right Alabama harmony, the exact right feeling I felt the first time I met that young lady. It wasn't overdubbed, overdone, or overanything.

My favorite Alabama album, if you were dying to know, is *Just Us,* which came out in the middle of the 1980s Alabama prairie fire, in 1987. This was a period when I was personally consumed with the possibility that we were making hit records one after another but in danger of losing our soul in the process. This one album helped me get over that worry. "Face to Face," off of that album, I wrote up in Dale Morris's office. I had this tune bouncing around in my head, a very romantic tune about two young lovers. I had the feeling, but I didn't quite have the line I needed to convey the depth of that feeling. I walked around with this problem for weeks, until I was up on the third floor of our house one night, and it came to me—the simple phrase "face to face." The fact is, the most important thing when making love to someone is that you are fulfilled with that person and want to look at him or her, face to face. If it's not there when you are face to face, then it's probably a one-night stand. It's not going to last long. As the song says, "We happen face to face."

Another song on that album that was a high mark for me
is "Falling Again," co-written by me, Greg Fowler, and Teddy. I
thought it was a hit from the moment we recorded it; Teddy was
not so sure. It ended up becoming the BMI Song of the Year, a
very prestigious award based on how many times a song is actually played on radio within a given time frame. It is the only song
I ever wrote that was given that award, and it is still a source of
considerable pride.

But the most personal song I wrote that ended up on *Just Us*,
in fact one of the most personal songs I've ever written, was "Tar
Top." Tar Top was a nickname given to me as a kid because of my
thick black head of hair. The song is 100 percent autobiographical, a look back to our Bowery days, and I originally conceived
of it as kind of a present to Teddy and Jeff and our early years
together. The central line is, "Where are you going, Tar Top?" It
was a question I often asked back then—"Where is this music
thing going to lead?"—and was still asking at the very height of
Alabama—"We're a hit, that's for sure, but where do we really
want to take this music?" It goes like this:

> *It was July hot 'cross Georgia*
> *On my way to Myrtle Beach*
> *I just got my diploma*
> *so I set out in search of me*
> *The honeymoon was over*
> *And Alabama was far away*
> *From being little more*
> *Than just a Southern state*

*I got a gig down at the Bowery*
*I played for tips and watered drinks*
*Just a novice in a business*
*That's seldom what it seems*

*And where are you going, Tar Top?*
*Where's J.C. and the Chosen Few?*
*I saw the Flash without T. Gentry*
*and B.V. left the Malibus.*

Those cryptic references in that last verse were touchstones
for all of us. Jeff Cook (J.C.) had a group called The Chosen Few.
Teddy (T. Gentry) once played with the previously mentioned
Bickerson Flash. Ben Vartanian (B.V.), our drummer in those
days, did his time with the Malibus.

Together we decided to put it out as a single, and it didn't
make it to the top. I think a lot of people kind of laughed at it,
never taking the time to stop and listen to the words and focus on
the imagery we were trying to evoke. The record company people
hated it. It was not their choice, and I don't think they exactly
went out of their way to make it a hit. It broke our string of consecutive hits at the time. The next song released, "Face to Face,"
hit No. 1, followed shortly by "Fallin' Again," another smash. "Tar
Top" was no hit, but to me it was one of the most important, and
memorable, songs we ever released.

Simply put, it wasn't a song that just anyone could sing. Only
we could do that song, because it was about our lives, our identity, our music. Many artists have songs so personal to them and
so identified with their lives that it's hard to imagine someone

else singing them. James Taylor's "Fire and Rain" comes to mind. It's about a special girl, Suzanne, and a specific event that only he truly understands. That's how I feel about "Tar Top."

And, for what it's worth, the video of "Tar Top" is, in my opinion, the best video we ever did. Directed by David Hogan, it has a special place in my heart because my son, Heath, all of four years old, is seen riding his bike in the video.

"Tar Top" and the album *Just Us* resolved a lot of my problems about getting too solely commercial for our own good. It helped me get past those singles that might have been good for Alabama, and all the people who made money off of Alabama, but really weren't *about* Alabama. I have never for a minute regretted all the success that Alabama was blessed to have, due largely to the people who bought our records and came to our shows. I would be the worst kind of ingrate if I felt any other way. I thank God in my prayers every night for all the good fortune He has given us, and I just hope I've done an adequate job of repaying Him and our public for their many gifts. I'm still working at it.

As the Alabama Express kept moving down the track and we turned the corner on the 1990s, the pressure, exhaustion, and constant, never-ending workload began to take its toll. The success didn't stop. From 1990 through 1993, we had another eleven No. 1 hits on country radio and kept up the grueling pace of hundreds of shows a year. If you look at one of Barbara's booking sheets from 1991, say, from March through the middle of December, it is a blur of inked-in scribbling of fifteen to twenty dates a month. In September, for instance, there are seventeen appearances scheduled, from York, Pennsylvania, to Jackson, Tennessee, and three days marked in big black letters, "Jeff off." I'm sure he was happy about that. I loved looking at that sheet and seeing, somewhere, "Randy off."

But, as Dale said, we were making hay while the sun was shining, and we knew this was a unique opportunity that might never come again. We weren't about to let anyone down or blow anyone off, from the fans in Rhinelander, Wisconsin, to Dick Clark. Every night we would go onstage and sing about many of the things we loved the best—the Tennessee River, family dinners at home, even playing for tips and watered down drinks—and occasionally we even got to go back home to remind ourselves about why we were working so hard. As crazy as life on the road could be—and it got plenty crazy—I was blessed to be grounded in the one sure thing in my life—a loving family.

# CHAPTER 7

# THE FAMILY

*Me and my woman's done made our plans*
*On the Tennessee River, walkin' hand in hand*
*Gonna raise a family, Lord, settle down*
*Where peace and love can still be found.*

"TENNESSEE RIVER" BY RANDY OWEN

Kelly remembers the exact moment when she knew our home
life was about to change and most likely change for good. We
were still living in the little brown house on Baugh Road with
the wood-burning stove for heat. Our daughter, Alison, born
in December of 1977, was about five, and our son, Heath, born
in 1981, was still an infant Kelly was carrying around on her hip.
The house, to repeat, was primitive. Besides having no heating
system, it had no insulation, and it was ice cold in the winter. The
wind came through the cracks in the floor and ceiling. Unless you
were huddled around the fire, you were miserable.

Our solution to this thorny problem was to nail old carpet wherever we could to cover those cracks. Teddy and I had worked at one point as carpet layers, and so we used our carpeting skills, I guess you'd say, to cover the walls in one bedroom and the kitchen with carpet scraps to keep out the cold. It looked a little weird—cheesy carpeting running up a wall like furry wall paper—but it did the trick. No one froze to death.

One other detail about that house worth mentioning was its TV setup. Kelly and I had bought a used color TV in Myrtle Beach from Don and Belle Tyler at the Century House, and since this was long before cable or satellite television, plus we lived way back in the woods, we had to erect an antenna on a long pole in the front yard. The problem was, the antenna had to be pointed in just the right direction to get the closest stations in the area—places like Chattanooga, Huntsville, or even Atlanta. Each of those locales demanded a different antenna position. If we wanted to watch the Atlanta news broadcast, say, Kelly or I would have to run outside in the cold and turn the pole toward Atlanta. It worked best when we were both at home—one of us could fiddle with the pole outside, while the other stayed inside and yelled, "A little farther that way, no, back the other way . . ." Then the pole turner would run back in, we'd snuggle up against the carpet walls, and watch TV.

Anyway, the day Kelly knew things had changed, she was out in the yard collecting pine kindling to start the fire in our stove. She would take an ax, find some pine knots growing on the trees in the nearby woods, and chip them off for kindling. It was 1982, and I was on the road damn near all the time. Alabama had been signed with RCA for a while by then, and the music was getting out there.

So Kelly was out front, fooling with the kindling, when a car pulled up and stopped. We didn't have a fence or any other kind of barrier around the house, and she felt a little vulnerable. These people got out, and Kelly said, "Hello, can I help you?" And they said, "Excuse us, but is this where Randy Owen with that group Alabama lives?" She had to say yes, of course, and be as nice as she could be, but at the same time in the back of her mind was the thought, *Oh, my God, if this is going to keep happening, I better figure out how to deal with it.* A big change, she knew, was coming.

Kelly had already gone through a whole series of difficult cultural changes just to get to this point in our life together. Just moving to Lookout Mountain and adapting to the ways of her in-laws there was a major transition for her. She had grown up in the suburbs of big cities and on military bases where everyone had air-conditioned houses, color TV, and a mall nearby to find anything you wanted. All of a sudden she is plopped into a fairly isolated, subsistence-based, highly religious community of people. She was used to going to bowling alleys, dance clubs, and drive-in theaters. They were used to church and weekend sing-ins of gospel music. They were two different worlds.

As I mentioned, Kelly moved in with my parents right after we got married, so she had no time to adjust to this radical shift in her life. My parents, for instance, got all their water from a well on their farm. They weren't tied in to the Fort Payne city water system. This meant that they had to ration the water they used because there wasn't an endless supply. Kelly was used to taking long, luxurious baths and, especially in hot weather, lingering in the shower, maybe two or three times a day, for as long as she wanted. That luxury was now gone, along with grabbing a beer from the refrigerator or dancing in the living room.

As she once admitted honestly, "In the year 1975, when we were married, I didn't know that people still lived like this."

That being said, Kelly clearly loved my parents and respected their ways and tried to help them in any way she could. She'd fix meals, work in the garden with Mama in the summer, and learned a lot from Mama about canning and freezing foods in the fall. On weekends she would travel with them to area churches when they performed as the Owen Family. And she learned to take five-minute showers.

But there were clearly differences between Kelly and my parents, from the way she dressed to her coming and going at her leisure, so we figured that the best way to keep peace in the family was to move to "the big city," Fort Payne, all of six miles away. We rented a tiny, one-bedroom apartment attached to a house owned by an older woman named Ethel Posy. This allowed Kelly a little more breathing space yet kept her within shouting distance of all my family up on the mountain. When I was gone, Kelly had Mrs. Posey to keep her company, as well as Teddy's wife, Linda, Jeff's wife, Josie, and Lynn Vartanian, the wife of our drummer, Bennett. They all lived down in Fort Payne back then.

We all adjusted to one another in time, as families normally do, and by the time we moved up to the little brown house, Kelly even learned a thing or two about living in the country and living with less, something my parents had done their whole lives. When you're living on well water and a woodstove, you naturally become more resourceful, from growing your own vegetables to entertaining yourself without running to the mall every five minutes. And as we started to have a family, we created our own self-defined life for ourselves and our kids and learned to live beside my family and yet maintain enough distance so as not to encroach on one another. This can be tricky sometimes, and a lot of young couples solve family conflicts by moving thousands of miles away, but this was unacceptable to me. We definitely wanted our kids to have the experience of knowing their grandparents, learning from them, and understanding the incredible value of being bonded to both our blood family and to the land.

Kelly, I must say, was remarkably grounded and self-sufficient for someone so young, let alone someone suddenly thrown into a completely different way of life. She called herself "a little home-body," something she relished. She was excited to have the kindling gathered and the TV antenna pointed in the right direction when Alabama got off the road and we had a weekend to ourselves. I guess she wanted to make sure I came back home and didn't get lost in the multiple distractions of a musician's life.

Early on, Kelly started getting the raised eyebrows and questioning looks when she told people that I was in Charlotte or New Orleans that night while she was sitting in a little brown house watching *Jeopardy*. "How can you just stay at home," someone would invariably ask, "while he's out there, traveling around, having all that fun? God, he's in the middle of a giant, movable party, and you're missing out!"

Her response was usually the question: "Excuse me, but do you go to work with your husband?" And they'd go, "Well, no." The point is, I was working. That was my job, pure and simple. If part of that assignment is having a good time at a nightclub, which it was, or dancing onstage or eating out with a local promoter or traveling to a new city and a new crop of fans, well, that's the job description. That's not the life Kelly chose for herself. She didn't sing, play the guitar, write songs, or want to be onstage. She was not trying to ride my coattails to her own musical stardom or celebrity fame. She was never looking for our family to do a reality TV show like Ozzie Osbourne or Gene Simmons. She wasn't shooting for the cover of *People*.

She rarely tells people, but Kelly never had the desire to go to college like our kids did. When we met, she taught dance and loved to dance and was focused on a career as a dance instructor. A competing interest to that, one that finally rose to the top, was the idea of living in the country and raising a family. One of her most endearing memories of her childhood was visiting her grandmother in rural Georgia and doing farm things like feeding chickens and helping with the dressing of the big hog that her grandmother would kill every year. And being second of a family of six kids, she was always taking care of youngsters. Early on she realized a fundamental truth about herself—she loved the simplicity of being at home, taking care of that home, being a wife and mother, and running a farm. This was her form of one woman's liberation.

Kelly claims that she has never resented my gadabout life. For one thing, she knows up close how unglamorous it often is. There's a good reason why we often refer to ourselves as "road dogs." Eighty some people, on the road constantly, walk into an empty hall, turn it into a hi-tech music show: we play, the crew tears it all down, and we go on to the next town. It's an exhausting routine. Half the time, we are literally dog-tired.

But the other reason Kelly doesn't envy my music life is because she feels what she's accomplished in motherhood is the equivalent to what I've accomplished in the music business. She has told our children that if she were dying, she could pass on knowing that she raised three wonderful kids. Three kids who know how to treat people and respect others, and who are humble and God-fearing. That was her job, and she pulled it off very well.

That attitude is a world or two away from the attitude of someone who feels entitled and superior to others because her husband sells a lot of records and appears on TV. As Kelly once said, "Our life would not have worked had I become a selfish mother, resenting my husband's fame and notoriety and trying to be in the limelight, which I've never done. So, you know, it worked for both of us. I feel like I'm a professional at what I did and am still doing, and he's definitely a professional at what he does."

Plus, Kelly loves the fact that old high-school friends from South Carolina, the ones who were so excited that she was going to marry a could-be country singing star, now tell her she hasn't really changed at all. To her, that is a high compliment. She never learned to play the stereotypical role of celebrity spouse. She may have aged a little, but her character and countenance remain as they always were. She's still the Kelly of the '60s and '70s, though she can now hang out backstage anytime she wants to.

Part of my own sense of being a professional, something again that goes back to the way I was raised, is that I try to keep my music life and my family life separate. I try to keep work away from home and home away from work. It's not always easy to do, but it is a healthy and necessary separation that I constantly strive to maintain. When I come home, I intend to have a good time being a father and husband, maybe even a better time than being the lead singer of Alabama. Growing up, the kids had little or no interest in the machinations of the music business and certainly wouldn't understand my obsession with it. They understood throwing a football around the front yard or hopping in the truck and seeing what the cows were up to. Families come and go among professional musicians, and the only way to keep one, I've come to learn, is to give it every bit as much time and attention as a career. This probably applies to a lot of other professions, too, but musicians are itinerant workers, moving from place to place, and that can put an incredible strain on a "normal" family life.

During all that time when they were growing up and Alabama was doing two or three hundreds dates a year, the stress was constant. But the truth is, when I got home, my kids would unstress me. It didn't matter to them if the record of the moment went to No. 1 or not. Or if the album of the moment went platinum, or whether or not we sold out the arena in Chicago. To them, it was simply a matter of Daddy's gone, but now Daddy's coming home! And we'd fool around and have a great time, a million miles away from the "business," and at night, the three of them would all get into bed with us, camped out on my arms. I'd be completely uncomfortable, but they'd be down for the night. And I can remember, at those moments, just looking at them and seeing how beautiful they were—how healthy and intelligent and grounded—and the accumulated stress of work would just fly out the window.

I didn't really see how they saw things until much later in life. We all figured out one day that each of the kids—Alison, born in the mid-'70s, Heath, born in the early '80s, and Randa, born in the late '80s—experienced one specific phase of the Randy Owen/Alabama story arc. Alison, who we call to this day Sissy, was the pre-Alabama kid—she remembers living in the trailer park in Myrtle Beach and taking a bath in a bucket. She remembers cold nights in the little brown house on the mountain. She remembers, at a tender young age, a story I told her about playing the song "It Never Rains in Southern California" forty straight times at a club in Fort McClellan, Alabama, one night because a military guy she describes as "a freak from Southern California" was missing home and willing to give us a tip every time we played it.

Alison, like the other kids, spent most of her growing-up years on Lookout Mountain and, like the others, considers hers a "normal" childhood. In her young mind, what I did for a living only slowly dawned on her. I was gone a lot, sure, but to her, I could have been in sales or marketing and had a lot of out-of-town customers. Heath and she thought it was fun when I came home. Kelly would pick me up at the local airport, and the two kids would hide in the back until we were halfway home, then jump out and scare me. Plus, Alison took her cues from her mom: "I never got sad when he was gone because Mom was always at home. She was fun and energetic, and we always had things like sports going on. And my mom didn't sit around saying, 'Oh, this is bad, this is so bad.'"

We made a conscious decision not to disrupt our kids' routines to accommodate the road. It was, as much as humanly possible, always the other way around. We rarely pulled them out of school to go on tour. They knew we took school seriously and that they should too. They might travel with us in the summer to a show or two, but not if it seriously interfered with set summer activities like sports. If there was a wall in my mind between work and reality, there was one in their minds too. This is what I do. This is where you live and what you do.

Inevitably, my public life slowly seeped into their private lives. Alison remembers being with me on one occasion when she was very young and a girl with purple hair with a pink stripe down the middle came up and said, "You're Randy Owen of Alabama, aren't you?" To Alison, it was a revelation that the purple-

172

haired crowd liked our music. She also remembers going to a
show in Birmingham when she was seven and holding the hand
of her Paw Paw Pyle. There was an opening act of some kind, and
Paw Paw said, "Boy, that was sure loud." Alison looked at him and
said, "Paw Paw, just wait until my dad comes out."

Alison has my overachieving genes, I guess. She lettered in
five sports at Fort Payne High School, was the class valedictorian,
received a basketball scholarship to Jacksonville State, and now
works in Nashville in the film-production business. Oh, yeah, she
also plays the guitar and writes songs.

In high-school sports, it was at best an irritant to have a
famous father. Some kid from another school would score on her
and then say, "Hey, how was that for some mountain music!" or
something less repeatable. The strangest moment for her came at
a state girl's basketball playoff game. With two minutes left in the
game, Alison's team was up by only two points, and things were
incredibly tense. Alison was on the sideline, about to throw the
ball inbounds to her teammates, when the referee holding the ball
looked over at her and asked, "Is your dad really Randy Owen?"
I guess this issue was pressing on his mind, and he needed an
answer before the game was over.

All my kids developed the strategy, once they knew what was
going on, of trying to keep their identities separate from mine,
at least upon meeting people for the first time. They did the very
opposite of what many celebrity kids might do, which would
be to announce who they are as a way of focusing attention on
themselves. My kids didn't want that added attention. If you

genuinely connect with someone and become friends, they'll find out soon enough. As Alison puts it, "A new friend will say, 'I really like that singer,' and I'll blurt out, 'Oh, yeah, she's really nice. I sat behind her at the American Music Awards.' Then it'll all come out, and she'll say, 'Why didn't you tell me?' And I'll say, 'Because I'd like you to know me before you know that.'"

In order to try out life without the complications of being Randy Owen's daughter, Alison moved to Atlanta for a few years to live on her own. She got a job at Seattle's Best Coffee and spent hours wandering around the attached Borders bookstore. She loved getting a job without someone saying, "Alabama? I love Alabama! You're hired!" In a multicultural, multinational city like Atlanta, just talking to the next customer walking in the door was an education. Now that she has relocated to Nashville, I guess you'd have to say she likes the city life.

Heath, born in 1981, got tagged early with the nickname Little Man, and it stuck. He never knew a time when Alabama wasn't big. Alison recalls the time when Heath was in kindergarten and we had an old Victorian house in Fort Payne where we lived at the time and still occasionally stay today. The house was right across the street from Heath's elementary school and allowed us to stay close to the kids' daily lives. One day as I was walking Heath from school, I noticed he was crying. I said, "Hey, what's wrong, son?" Heath took a long breath, then said, "Those boys over there said they were glad you didn't win that award last night!"

You can imagine what it would be like to grow up on display. Heath remembers, not too long after kindergarten, when he was out in our big front yard playing catch with Alison, and they looked up and saw ten or fifteen cars parked along the road right outside the fence of the yard. Dozens of people piled out of the cars and lined up along the fence, waving and shouting and snapping pictures as fast as they could. Heath's reaction: "There's something weird going on here."

The first time the weirdness really hit him, he claims, was on a family trip to Disney World. It was 1983, and I had decided, in my then-naive fashion, that it was time to take a family vacation. Heath, all of two or three, was up on my shoulders as we were leaving the Polynesian Resort to spend the day on Main Street, USA. No sooner had we entered the lobby than what to him looked like thousands of Japanese tourists surrounded us. They all recognized me at once and began to press in for a better look and a Kodak memory. Heath went berserk. It was like a horror movie to him, and was not that much different to me. As he bawled, we hustled him back to the elevator and away from the crowd. So much for a quiet family vacation.

Heath, like Alison, never introduces himself as, "Hi, I'm Heath Owen, son of Randy Owen." He hates the preconceived notions people have about what he should be like as the son of a celebrity. People assume he will be arrogant, self-absorbed, flashy, throwing money around, and spoiled. Turn on TV and that's what you see. I'm sure those Hollywood stereotypes do a disservice to a lot of kids whose parents just happen to be actors or performers. They have nothing to do with my kids.

Heath prefers to meet people who *don't* know who Alabama is, but he grew up here and now lives and works in Nashville, like

Alison, so there aren't a whole lot of people around who fit that bill. His favorite story about Growing Up Owen took place while he was a starter on the varsity baseball team at Samford University in Birmingham. Heath had aspirations at one point of playing in the majors and was even invited to tryouts with the Cardinals and the Cubs. Unfortunately, like a lot of young players, he suffered a career-ending injury before he even had a career.

In any case, while playing college ball at Samford, the team would play the University of Alabama Crimson Tide every year on their home field in Tuscaloosa. And every year, without fail, Heath would step up to the plate and out of the PA system would come an Alabama song, played at maximum volume. The home-town crowd would go nuts, thinking this was the cleverest way to taunt and rattle an opponent ever invented. Heath thought it was dumb and tacky, which it was.

At his last game at U of A, Samford beat the Tide, and Heath had a really good day, going two for three with two doubles. At his last at-bats in that game, when the music started up yet again, it was all he could do to keep from turning to the crowd, taking a bow, and flipping them off. He held himself in check. He didn't want to come off as the smart-ass son of a famous singer.

Randa, now a sophomore at Auburn University in Auburn, Alabama, got the biggest share of the late-Alabama or post-Alabama view of my life. As with all of them, I tried to arrange my schedule so I wouldn't miss a baseball or football game or a school play. With Randa, a lover of livestock and animal husbandry, I wouldn't miss one of her beauty pageants or cattle shows. "Punk," we call her, as in the sitcom character Punky Brewster. And Punk loves the country life.

Growing up when she did, Randa is a little mystified by all the star talk. People ask her what it's like to have a famous dad who goes on tour all the time, and her answer is: "I look at them, and I'm like, you know, he's my dad. He goes to my football and softball and basketball games, you know, like a dad. He's a shoulder to cry on; he'll call you up and give you hell if you get out of line. Sure, he goes on tour and performs onstage and sings with all these amazing artists, but at the end of the day, he comes home. And he's just my dad."

My bonding time with Randa is on the ranch. She loves the fact that I can be on the phone with a music producer one minute, then hang up and the next minute be examining a cow and talking about pedigrees. I love that too. I love having a daughter who finds the cattle business as rewarding and relaxing as I do.

One of Randa's fondest memories of being with me, and one of mine, too, occurred at the Alabama State Junior Heifer and Steer Show just last year. It was her last year to show because she was about to graduate high school and become ineligible. She had started showing at eleven, and I remember how excited I was that at least one of my kids had a passion similar to my own boyhood passion and of course my daddy's lifelong passion.

In any case, it was her last year, her last shot, and she was showing a Hereford mixed-breed steer, called a Hereford Influenced steer, named Romeo. And she won! Romeo brought home the blue ribbon. And as Randa remembers it, as she stood out there in the show ring, I came running out and grabbed her and gave her the tightest hug I'd ever given her. I don't doubt it. It was such a proud moment for me. With my help, mostly cheerleading, she accomplished something she had set out to do, and I couldn't have been more thrilled. Randa says we just stood out there forever until other people started to stare at us like we were a little crazy. I couldn't have cared less.

Randa, a.k.a. Punk, won National Champion Hereford Heifer this year at Kansas City and is now majoring in animal science at Auburn with an eye on becoming a veterinarian. Like both Alison and Heath, she is out there pursuing her own dreams, in the same way I did when I took off for South Carolina after college, and here's hoping they all reach them.

Randa's interest in all things country as a kid only helped reenforce all the pleasure I got from having a different work life on the ranch away from the demands of the music business. From our days in Myrtle Beach, Kelly and I would come home on weekends and hop in the pickup truck and take hay to my daddy's cattle. They were commercial cattle—stockyard cattle—but he loved to tend to them, and so did we. My dream, as I mentioned, was to be able to buy him some registered cattle to own and swap. After he died, I decided to fulfill that dream in part by going into the cattle business myself.

Kelly and I started with three registered Herefords and built the business from that. We now have six hundred head of Herefords and Angus plus a number of crossbred cattle. I profit from this enterprise in so many ways that go beyond money.

It connects me to the land. It connects me to the rhythm of the seasons and the life cycles of the animals, to the memory of my daddy, and now to my children and the legacy of this mountain property I hope to pass on to them and their children. And the cows don't care who I am. If I don't feed them and take care of them, they are going to bawl.

And my dogs didn't care who I was, either. Two of the most memorable dogs we had during this period were two bulldog puppies named Pooterst and Chillynx, a tribute to the imaginary friends Reba and I had as kids. Chillynx, the female, didn't get along too well with humans, but Pooterst, the male, was one of the most beloved animals in my whole life. Then he wandered away one day and broke my heart. I offered no less than a $10,000 reward for his return. When I got no takers, I offered the same amount for even information about his whereabouts. No one ever stepped up.

During the constant comings and goings of Alabama, I tried to invent ways where I could stay close to home and still keep the music coming. One of the best ideas we came up with was the June Jam.

The June Jam was a one-day, outdoor, multiartist music festival—all for charity—we began staging annually every June in Fort Payne starting in 1980. After it got rolling, it was a regular lollapalooza. Over the next sixteen summers, it turned into the biggest continuous outdoor charity event ever staged, certainly in country music, and maybe ever will be. It was one long sixteen-year party.

The event started out on the wrong foot, as things often do. A promoter called us to say he wanted to put on a concert in Fort Payne and give all the money to charity. We showed up and did our part, and he disappeared. I'm not sure where any of the money went. We didn't like to see the community burned like that, not to mention our being tricked, so we decided to continue the event and run it ourselves. That way we could invite artist friends to participate, and they knew they weren't about to be sucker-punched.

The first June Jam took place in the Fort Payne High School football stadium. As it grew, anywhere from fifty to eighty thousand people would show up to fill this converted hay and practice field adjacent to the high school. Overnight, a huge, free-standing, multitiered, two-stage set would spring up. Greg Fowler once said it was like "standing on the deck of the *Enterprise*." The onslaught of people and stars would take over the town of Fort Payne for that period, much like the Woodstock Festival took over the small community of Bethel in Upstate New York. This was a Southern Woodstock for the whole family.

At its height in the mid to late 1980s, June Jam was a huge operation, one that demanded its own staff apart from our crew that was on the road full-time with the band. It involved coordinating the schedules and demands of dozens of artists to come and perform—for free—as well as all the logistics in accommodating these huge crowds. Gaynelle Pitts, formerly our fan-club president, ran the show year-round with the tireless help of Denise Stegner, production manager Brent Barrett, stage coordinator Ed Turner, and big Steve Boland, our longtime road manager, running interference. The long weekend usually started with the annual VIP softball game—the band and crew would be one team; pro players, celebrities, and local politicians, the other. Then there would be the Randy Owen Celebrity Golf Tournament. There was also a parade through the middle of downtown Fort Payne, plus tours of the Alabama Museum in town, fan-club get-togethers, a special Gospel Jubilee performance, and Jeff's fishing tournament.

On concert day we would have two fully-rigged stages going at once, with the most sophisticated setup imaginable. At one point we had to bring in closed-circuit TV so a band waiting in their bus could see when an act onstage was wrapping up so they could get ready to perform. There was never any reset time between acts. When one performer finished on stage one, another started up on stage two, and all the people in the field had to do was reposition their blankets or lawn chairs.

The greatest names in country music showed up year after year to play for free and help us raise money for area charities: Alan Jackson, Charlie Daniels, Vince Gill, Garth Brooks. When Willie Nelson came to perform, he showed up with a broken hand. He had apparently injured it in a bicycle accident just before the concert date. Thousands of people had come to the event just to see Willie, who is renowned for doing long, three-to-four-hour jam sessions onstage. I went to his bus that day and said, "Willie, we are so honored to have you here, and a lot of people specifically came to see you. Would you mind playing for at least an hour?" He said, "An hour? Sure, no problem," and went onstage and did a fantastic hourlong set, broken hand and all.

Among the most anticipated appearances at June Jam were Dolly Parton and Billy Ray Cyrus at the point when "Achy Breaky Heart" was the hottest song in country music. Only two performers in the sixteen-year history of the Jam asked for payment, and I won't tell you who they were. You have to remember that this event took place right in the middle of summer, the busiest touring season of the year for any performer. Alan Jackson or Garth Brooks could have been playing some giant arena for serious money. Instead, that night, they were playing in a hay field in Fort Payne for free.

We coordinated the schedule of June Jam to occur around the same time as Fan Fair, the giant gathering of stars and fans in Nashville. That way people could drive down for the day, or our plane would fly them down, and then head back that night if they wanted. Other fans camped out in Fort Payne, filled up every area motel room from Gadsden to Chattanooga, and through the good graces of local citizens, parked in driveways and slept in front yards.

The June Jam was the biggest ongoing performance of the year for Alabama, even when we were at our very hottest. One year we had twenty-eight acts perform on one day. It was like going to the CMA awards and every nominee in the audience got onstage to perform.

There's a travel video on YouTube that gives the feel of the event—aerial shots of tens of thousands of fans sitting in the hot sun, little kids riding on floats in the parade down Main Street,

Marty Stuart or Charlie Daniels or Wayne Newton onstage, me in the shortest of short shorts (very fashionable in the 1980s) getting thrown out at home plate in the softball game. As the video concludes, "What better way to spend a few days in June?"

Over the years, we were able to raise over $4 million for charity through June Jam proceeds and gave most of it away close to home. We helped underwrite many improvements at the football field at Fort Payne High School, gave much-needed funds to area fire and police departments, and helped revive school music programs being cut from school budgets everywhere in and around Alabama. One year we gave $68,000 to the local school system so that kids could get new math books.

We also set up a program for granting individual scholarships to worthy kids to be able to go on to college. I took charge of this end of things and loved the interaction with possible recipients. I'm not great with names, but I'll never forget the kid who was the co-valedictorian of his high-school class but was actually homeless. He wanted to be the best naval officer ever. Or the girl who walked into my office in a dirty dress with lint all over it, a sure sign she had to work in the sock mills to help her family. She was third in her high-school class and dreamed of college, but her American father had passed away, her Japanese mother could barely speak English, and she looked completely defeated. I got her a start-up scholarship to Northeast Alabama Community College, and the next time she came in to apply for a full scholarship, she was dressed up, ready to tackle the world. It was a stunning transformation.

For most of its duration, the June Jam event had the whole-hearted support of the local officials and people of Fort Payne. But after sixteen years it finally came to an end for a variety of reasons but principally because the mayor and his staff at that time thought it was too much of a burden for a small town to handle. To us this was both baffling and hurtful. We were bringing millions of dollars of business into the area every June, not to mention the highest-paid country performers on earth, and they saw it as one big drain on city services like street cleaning and garbage collection. They increasingly made life miserable for us, we had a parting of the ways, and in 1997 the June Jam went dark.

But the spirit of June Jam still lives on through two operations: the Alabama June Jam escrow account, a way of continuing to dole out proceeds to worthy organizations, and the annual June Jam Songwriters Showcase, a place for accomplished songwriters to expose their work to the public. In 2008, the showcase took place at the Northeast Community College in Rainsville, my alma mater, and all proceeds went to John Croyle's Big Oak Ranch for boys and girls, three separate Northeast Alabama facilities for abused, neglected, and wayward children.

So my steadfast partner in life, Kelly, my growing family, the cattle business, and music-related events like the June Jam kept me close to home and for the most part grounded in a place and a way of life I understood. But, that said, breaks at home didn't completely eliminate the pressures of Alabama. Our ascendancy from Holiday Inns to traveling two hundred or more days a year

was so fast and our commercial success so constant and pro-
longed that the stress was clearly building, even though I was so
focused on the job at hand that I wasn't all that aware of it.

 I was aware, of course, that I often had to say yes to some
commitment or some marketing strategy or even some soon-to-
be hit song when I wanted to say no. I was aware that I was one
of a band of four who spent untold hours together, on and off
stage, who didn't always see eye to eye on things, but who had to
keep working as a unit for the sake of the whole enterprise, an
enterprise responsible for the livelihoods of dozens of people.
And I was aware that once I left the mountain, I had no privacy
and no real freedom to go somewhere with the family and be left
alone. I could see these distinct day-to-day pressures, but I wasn't
cognizant of the bigger picture and the cumulative effect of those
multiple sources of tension.

Kelly, at a slight distance, could see things building much
better than I could, but then again, the Alabama phenomena was
as new to her as it was to me. At some point, under this kind of
constant pressure, something had to give. And that something
was my health.

# CHAPTER 8

# BREAKDOWN

*Now there's a sad lookin' moon*
*Shinin' down on me*
*There's a sad lookin' sky*
*As far as I can see*

"SAD LOOKIN' MOON" BY RANDY OWEN, TEDDY
GENTRY, AND GREG FOWLER

By the early 1990s, I was sitting on top of the flagpole. The whole group was up there, in fact, and looking back, I don't think this was something that was widely acknowledged in the media at large. Our fans knew who we were, as did country radio, every aspiring writer of country songs, and the country-music business in general. Dick Clark and the American Music Awards sure knew who we were, along with the Country Music Awards, the Academy of Country Music Awards, and the Grammys. We had won the CMA Entertainer of the Year three times in a row in the 1980s and the ACM Entertainer of the Year five years in a row, and to top off the decade, we were awarded the prestigious ACM award for Artist of the Decade in 1989.

We had sold a lot of records and walked across a lot of award stages by then, but we really weren't heralded in the mainstream media for many of our accomplishments. We were well on our way to becoming one of the top twenty best-selling popular music acts *of all time* and all genres, but I doubt if too many people who weren't big country music fans knew that. In many ways, we operated under the radar of the national press.

The reason for this is probably pretty simple. We didn't cause scandals, the mother's milk of the entertainment media. We weren't seen out partying in New York or Los Angeles or throwing furniture out of a hotel window in Paris. We didn't move to Nashville or participate in the publicity-generating social world there. We didn't have public fallings-out or lawsuits or hateful tit for tats in the *National Enquirer*. We were three working musicians who did our job, gave great attention to our fans, then went home to Fort Payne and tried to lead normal lives. We were big business, but we were a very grounded operation. Success in the entertainment business and notoriety in the tabloid press are not the same thing. You never saw a picture of me, with a hat pulled over my head, sneaking out of the Betty Ford Center.

When you're on top of the flagpole, you get pulled in a lot of directions. People want you to show up at their fund-raising events, come to their inaugural balls, talk to their morning drive-time radio DJs at six in the morning, be in their newspapers, and even sing at their weddings. A reporter from a Birmingham newspaper casually dropped in on my mama one day, chatted with her for a while, asked her a lot of questions, then published a big feature story about her. She considered it a complete affront to her privacy that anyone would do such a thing. I always saw stuff like that, at least when directed toward me, as just part of the job, but sometimes all the personal appearances and other demands on your time become the job itself, and the music almost becomes what you do between all the other "must appears" on your schedule.

The one way I've always dealt with stress was with stress of another kind. I could get rid of a lot of the emotional and psychological stress with the physical stress of performing or, when I wasn't in the performing mode, with good old-fashioned exercise. Doing a three-hour show in front of twenty thousand people is definitely a workout. I don't just stand there onstage with a guitar, singing and smiling. I'm jumping around, singing loud, taking off one sweaty T-shirt and pulling on another, and in general putting on a show, and it can be very physically demanding. I would often walk off the stage having lost four or five pounds just in sweat alone. I felt like Chipper Jones after a playoff game. Performing is definitely an athletic exercise.

I look forward to it and always have, because I always feel good after a big show. I'm exhausted, but I'm also exhilarated. After a few years of this kind of aerobic work, I realized that the healthier I was when walking *onto* the stage, the better I felt afterward. I didn't start out to be heath conscious. It just turned out that way. Which was another reason drugs and alcohol never appealed to me much. They might offer one form of pleasure, but they definitely detracted from another form, the pleasure of pushing myself onstage. My parents never had a drink of alcohol or an upper or a snort of coke in their lives, but some of my extended family weren't so pure—a few of them both abused alcohol and were abusive because of it. Let's put it this way—I never met a drinker or drug consumer who was a *good* role model for the practice.

Using stress to eliminate stress was a healthy thing to do, and I increasingly tried to benefit from living and eating right, but it wasn't a magic pill. In retrospect, it seems I could not have avoided what now looks like an inevitable crisis. Kelly calls it the Big Kahuna.

It came in May of 1994. One evening, we flew back to Nashville from Los Angeles after the annual ACM Awards. Dale had an old car he let us use occasionally, so I decided to drive from Nashville to Fort Payne so I could once again sleep in my own bed. As I drove home, I felt completely exhausted and was probably dehydrated, though frankly at the time I didn't really know what "dehydrated" meant. I just knew I needed rest.

In bed that night, I was abruptly awakened by one of the commercial jets headed for the Hartsfield International Airport in Atlanta. Atlanta is ninety miles away, but the jets heading east get pretty low when they fly over the high point of Lookout Mountain and can sometimes be so loud they almost knock you out of your bed. See, even way up here in Northeast Alabama, you can't quite escape from civilization.

When that jet woke me up out of a dead sleep, my heart was beating very fast. It definitely frightened me, especially since long after the noise was gone, it was still beating at a dangerously high rate. Kelly awoke and said that I had "a real funny, pasty color." I told her I thought I was having a heart attack. She took my pulse. It was sky-high.

Kelly called a friend of ours who was a registered nurse, and she told us we should head down to the ER at the local hospital in Fort Payne. We did as told, but when we got there, the hospital staff went into such high gear that it scared the hell out of me all over again. They were just doing their job—looking for signs of a heart attack or some other kind of pulmo-cardiac malfunction—but since they had no instant answers, I stayed stressed. They hooked me up to an IV, gave me a stress test, ordered up some nitroglycerine to expand my blood vessels, and concluded there was no apparent sign of a heart attack.

The next morning we made the decision to go to Birmingham to see a cardiologist for a more definitive diagnosis. There they administered an arteriogram, or angiogram, an X-ray test where they use a special dye to see how blood flows through your heart and arteries. During the procedure, I could hear the doctors talking about my heart canals and arteries, and I remember one doctor saying, "Well, that one's perfect. I bet the other's the same way."

Under the anesthetic they had administered, it seemed to me that the lead cardiologist, Dr. Randy Harrison, had eyes as big as saucers. That worried me. *Maybe the other one* wasn't *the same way,* I thought. Then Dr. Harrison said, "Your heart is fine, Randy. In fact, it's really something. Your arteries look like a baby's arteries."

"Is that good?" I asked, anxiously.

"Yes," Dr. Harrison said, "really good."

Apparently my problem wasn't a damaged heart. His advice was simple: if you want to go fishing, go fishing. If you want to go hunting, go hunting. Exercise if you want. But if you're off to exercise or hunt or fish and someone wants to stop you and distract you with some urgent matter, that person is not your friend. "Don't stop," he said, "to talk to people and be responsible for everything that's going on in the world. If you continue to stop every time to solve every problem that comes along, you're going to end up destroying yourself."

So I didn't have a heart attack, it turns out. I had an attack of exhaustion, both mental and physical but probably more mental than physical. That doctor did me a huge favor. He explained what was obvious to him: my body was shutting down.

By this time word had gotten out that something was wrong with Randy Owen. The media started showing up at the hospital, and Greg Fowler, along with a very competent public-information staff on-site, had to step in and run interference. Kelly remembers being in the hospital room and looking up at the TV newscaster reporting, "Randy Owen has apparently suffered a heart attack." We had to dodge the cameras and stamp out those kinds of reports at the same time that we were alerting Nashville to what was actually going on. Whatever Alabama had scheduled in the coming days wasn't going to happen. As I mentioned before, a lot of people, probably in excess of a hundred or more, were now dependent on the band for a salary check, but I had to let that thought go for once. I was hospitalized until the doctors told me differently.

Kelly then did something she rarely did in the last two decades of nonstop Alabama-related obligations and appointments. She stepped up and said no. "I've never stood in the way before," she let it be known, "but I'm standing in the way today."

As the doctors explained, I was exhausted, worn out, spent. Remaining in this state could lead to something much worse, like a stroke or genuine heart failure. I now thank God this emergency happened, because it was clearly an early warning of more dire consequences to come. And if you are of the mind-set where you feel superresponsible and superdriven to make sure everything, all the time, is satisfactory and smooth sailing to a roomful of people—that is a difficult mental habit to break. It's probably a harder habit to break than a drug habit, though I've never had the latter. It was not selfish for me to start thinking about taking care of myself. It was mandatory.

We stayed in the hospital for a couple of days, often trying to convince people who dropped by that the problem wasn't my heart—in fact, had never been my heart—but my pace and my attitude. Still, some people didn't quite understand. If I was just tired, they concluded, then all I needed was a little bed rest and I'd be back on the same schedule. Otherwise, I'm dragging my feet. It got to the point where if someone from the business side called me at home, Kelly would tell the person she wasn't even going to give me the message. When someone said, "Oh, there's nothing really wrong with him," that person could only hope that Kelly wasn't within hearing distance, or they'd catch some serious blowback. Without her at that time, I don't know what I would have done.

You can begin to resent it when you feel you're being misunderstood like that, or worse, taken for granted. It works on your insides, breeding anger, self-doubt, and depression. That's exactly how I began to feel: resentful.

You can ask anyone—Dale, Kelly, Greg, anyone—and each will tell you I was not the easiest person to be around in the period following that scare. I tried to withdraw and understand what my body was trying to tell me at the same time others were trying to pull me back into the endless routine and worries that had put me in the hospital in the first place. It was a clear and plain disconnect between what I felt inside and what was expected of me outside, and I hated it. I was more than out of sorts—I was in a state of mental pain and confusion—and it was best to keep your distance. I was on a short fuse.

As Kelly has remarked, there was the added pressure of everyone thinking that because three of us were cousins, Alabama as a group always got along and, as she says, "were happy, happy, happy all the time," and that of course just wasn't true. We didn't make a point of airing our differences in public, but we had them, for sure, and in this period, I took it all very personally.

Dale remembers how difficult it was, or should I say, how difficult I was. "It got to be," he now recalls, "where Randy would go out and perform, and I'd make a special effort to come to the show, and he wouldn't even see me at his dressing room afterward. He completely cut me off. He wasn't seeing anybody. And, boy, that killed me. Because, you know, you feel like you're the father of this troupe, trying to take care of everything, and you feel that coming back at you. It was tough. It was tough on all of us."

Barbara Hardin is even more blunt. "He was funky and mean, but we just loved him anyway. He was mean as hell. He didn't speak to any of us for like three months. They were playing at Opryland that year, and I would just show up every night anyway. I'd just stand in the corner and smile at him so he'd know I was still there."

Kelly contends that I was the first one to go down in the group because I was the one who felt *too* responsible all the time. "Hell," she would say to me, "maybe you should think about doing a little more drinking and acting up, and that way you might be still out there running around. Maybe a bad habit like that would be good for you. You might just miss one of those all-important meetings you never miss now."

The kids had to experience all of this as well. Heath saw the uncertainty in my outlook. "When he had the panic attack, it was one of those things where he was down because he really didn't know what to expect. He was worried about what might be next. Is this just a prelude to something much worse about to happen?"

Whatever the source, I was emotionally raw, that's for sure, and withdrawn and unpleasant and surly and quick to anger and, in general, one unpleasant bastard. During this dark episode, I began to realize something I never really thought about for the preceding fourteen years. It wasn't just the pressure of the business or the disagreements with the other people in the band that was pushing me over the edge. It was also something I had failed to do for a decade and a half—mourn the loss of my father.

It made perfect sense. My daddy had died suddenly of a massive heart attack. In the midst of this overpowering career of mine, I had what I thought was a massive heart attack. I felt the connection, deeply, before I was ever conscious of it. It was also like I had to experience, in some way, what he had experienced to feel the full measure of his loss.

The people who knew me best could see this, and that probably helped them see beyond my sullen behavior. Dale, to whom I was and still am extremely close, saw this clearly. He called that mourning period "just about the saddest thing I've ever seen." It was painful for him to watch and painful for me to endure. I guess the grief, and maybe the guilt, had been building up for all those supersuccessful years, and it just had to come out when I hit the wall like that. Grieving takes time—it is not something you can simply turn on and off like a light switch. I had to learn that lesson in the worst of circumstances, when few people around me understood and a lot of close associates simply needed me to carry on with the show.

When a person is in a state like this, inevitably a doctor will suggest medication of some sort. Something my parents would never consider—have a problem? take a pill—is now the way most of us live. I was clearly suffering from some sort of depression, perhaps even a bipolar condition, and I had a lot of trouble sleeping. I signed up for a series of medications but didn't feel right about it. Kelly and I began to educate ourselves as to the possible downside of these drugs, and the more I learned, the queasier I felt about becoming dependent on them to sleep, to calm down, or anything else. Later, after the tragic death of actor Heath Ledger, I saw that three or four of the meds he had been taking had been prescribed to me as well. One was Xanax, another Inderol. At the time, I took them and hoped they would bring me out of my funk. I was wrong.

I remember being at the June Jam that year and feeling really out of sorts and difficult to be around. *Why do I feel this way?* I kept asking myself. It took me awhile, and some insight from the books we read, before I realized I didn't need these medications and they were in fact counterproductive. I felt bad. They made me feel even worse.

Again, it was by God's mercy, by the help of someone watching over me or praying for me, that I made the decision to pitch them into the wastebasket. I kept remembering what the doctors in Birmingham told me. Because I never smoked and had always done physical labor, my arteries were healthy, my heart strong, and my blood pressure low. One doctor said he wished his blood pressure was as low as mine. There's no reason, they said, that I needed to do anything other than rest and stop carrying the weight of Alabama on my shoulders. So that's what I tried to do, despite all the depressing and angry moods I fell into. I waited it out, you might say, and never developed any dependence on prescription drugs that often ends up controlling a lot of good people's lives.

In the process, I developed a more skeptical view of doctors, a view my parents always had. The sad part is that doctors are some of the most wonderful and big-hearted people in the world. But they are also people who can give you things that might end up killing you, if you don't watch it. Your health is your responsibility. They are just your medical advisers.

I switched from doctors who treat ailments to a wellness doctor, one who helps me design the right way to live and keep away from self-induced practices that would impair my health. I like to protect myself against illness instead of simply waiting until it happens. That's a critical lesson I learned during this bad stretch—take your own health seriously, and maintain a watchful eye over habits, including the habit of working too hard, that can only lead to trouble. I believe it's a sin to go out and just try to kill yourself, and I don't plan on doing it anytime soon.

Now, at the advice of my wellness doctor, I have a glass or two of wine when I want to. It's not something I grew up doing, but there are genuine health benefits to wine, not to mention the taste. In fact, as I write this, I am planning to start my own vineyard up here on Lookout Mountain. I'd love for my daddy to be around so I could toast him with the first glass of Owen-produced wine.

It took me a couple of years to come out of this whole episode, all the time touring and recording, and outside of a small group of people, no one had any idea about what was really going on. I didn't write a book about becoming burned out at forty-four or waiting fourteen years to grieve for my beloved dad, then going on *Oprah* to talk about it. I prayed and kept working. By this point Alabama had at least thirty-six No. 1 hit records, and the touring and recording demands were still intense. We were a well-oiled touring machine, a small group of professionals—from the players onstage to the extremely proficient and creative people backstage—and despite my being, in Barbara's words, "mean as hell," we kept moving forward.

The next turning point probably came the summer I decided I wanted Kelly and the kids on the road with me. It was toward the end of summer, well after school let out. They probably spent a month with me on tour, going on a big Midwestern swing through places like Michigan and South Dakota, and it was wonderful. We had never traveled as a family like that. I had never come off stage in a distant city, night after night, to see the four of them waiting for me in the wings. Alison was a junior in high school by then, Heath was a freshman, and "Punk" was still a punky five or six.

That extended family adventure, I think, was the occasion where my bad feelings about my life started to fade and I began to feel almost normal again. Whatever healing I had needed, physical or mental, had slowly happened, and I was ready to resume the responsibilities of my career without resentment or reservation. I may have been less malleable after that and much less anxious to make sure that everything was hunky-dory all the time. From 1996 until we decided on staging the American Farewell Tour in 2003, Alabama kept up a rigorous schedule of touring and recording, and I did a much better job of balancing that work with other passions in my life.

Barbara has said that she thinks Kelly and I are the most grounded people she has ever met. I don't know about that, but I clearly lost my footing during that period and became as un-grounded as I have ever been. Again, I thank God and Kelly and everyone else for allowing me to stumble around until I regained my equilibrium. I'd say I'm the better for it.

Kelly feels that I got stronger through that experience, and she is probably right. I had a much better grasp of how I was going to conduct myself going forward, protect myself from the pitfalls and pressures of this life, and preserve my energy for the important things like performing and my ever-increasing charity work. Kelly says I even sounded more powerful onstage: "It was not like somebody who had been reborn, but just somebody who had really gotten a new strength, spiritual as much as physical, and was now totally committed to using it. He certainly didn't lay back—in fact, I've never seen the man lay back. He just had a whole new way of doing things."

Kelly has a saying—"It's hard to hide real people." What that means, I think, is that your real nature is going to come out in some way, whether you're trying to hide it, even from yourself. "Real" people simply accept this fact and try not to disguise who they are with pretense, money, fame, drugs, alcohol, or any other diversion. You get up, and you are what you are. Otherwise, as someone said, when you're not yourself, you have to go around remembering who you were when other people said they liked you. It's a simple lesson—drop the idea that you have to be all things to all people all the time. We are all imperfect. If you screw up, fine. You're not alone.

I knew we weren't finished with what we set out to do with Alabama, and I knew I would forever feel bad if I just gave in to the pressure and quit. Or gave into the pressure and let myself go. By the mid–'90s, we were certainly back in high gear, and as I said, few people knew there was even a slight pause in our momentum. "Staying Power" read the cover of *Country Weekly* in June of 1997, summing up our then seventeen years on top and more No. 1 hits like "Give Me One More Shot" and "She Ain't Your Ordinary Girl."

By the end of the decade we had been recognized in ways unimaginable to anyone in the music business and especially to this group of four self-trained musicians—Jeff on lead guitar, Teddy on bass, Mark on drums, and me on lead vocals—who had remained a solid unit since 1980, through thick and thin.

In 1998 we got our star implanted on the Hollywood Walk of Fame. If you want to step on us, just go to 7060 Hollywood Boulevard in L.A., just east of La Brea Avenue, and look down on the sidewalk.

In 1999, RIAA, the trade group that represents the entire recording industry in the United States, the official body that certifies gold and platinum records, gave Alabama the award for Country Group of the Century. Such an honor is really hard to fathom. I guess they have to wait another hundred years to give out the next one.

I think that going through that awful period and coming out in decent shape made me more comfortable in my own skin, but I also think it gave me a much greater appreciation of what others who suffer must feel, and especially those who suffer in much worse ways than I did. Some historians have said that Franklin Roosevelt became sensitized to the lives of poor people by becoming paralyzed from polio. I think I became more sensitized to, say, children who suffer from cancer, by my comparatively lesser struggle with anxiety and depression. And this might not have happened if I hadn't hit that wall.

Part of the continuing mission of Alabama, I began to feel even more strongly, was to use the group's public profile as a jumping-off point to help people who were down and may never get up the rest of their lives. While the love and appreciation you get from fans is genuine and gratifying, there is a love you get from face-to-face contact with people in need that is incomparable. And I have never found this truer than in my nearly twenty-year association with a place in Memphis called St. Jude.

# CHAPTER 9

# GIVING BACK

*I saw the time*
*When special kids got a chance*
*And the handicapped could advance*
*I saw the time*
*When we walked the streets without risks*
*And families still prayed, and hugged, and kissed*
*I saw the time*

"I SAW THE TIME" BY RANDY OWEN

Part of the Alabama story, from its very inception, has always been about extending ourselves beyond the business of music and using our name to raise money, raise consciousness, and try to genuinely help the community around us. As a group, we have our collective causes, like the June Jam and the Celebrity Softball Game to aid the Big Oak Ranch, and we each have our separate interests as well. And we've been more than recognized for this work, culminating in a great honor for us, the Minnie Pearl Award for outstanding humanitarian and community contributions, given by *Country Weekly* and TNN in 2000.

We are far from alone in the country-music community in building charity work into our lives. There's a reason why the June Jam could get twenty-eight major artists to show up to play for free for one concert in the middle of touring season. Probably more than with any other branch of American music, country performers feel the calling to help others. From Willie Nelson's Farm Aid to Vince Gill's work with kids with drug and alcohol problems to Tim McGraw and Faith Hill's presence on the scene the minute Hurricane Katrina hit the Gulf Coast—reaching out to others is built into the ground-level connection between country artists and their audience, I think. Country stars, most of whom come from humble roots, have a particular affinity for the needs of common people.

I have always been involved in charity work of some kind since we left the Bowery in Myrtle Beach. As we were speeding through the 1980s, in addition to the Jams and golf tournaments and working with the state of Alabama on trying to help farming and farmers, we were constantly bombarded with requests from very worthy charities trying to get our support and involvement. There was no way any of us could have answered all their calls for help and have time for anything else, like making music and giving concerts. I'm sure that if I had wanted to, I could have spent every day of the year appearing somewhere to raise much-needed money for somebody. When I hit the wall in the early '90s, I had to learn to say no to people I just didn't have the time or energy to help. As time went on, my work in this area became more and more focused on the situations with which I had a deep emotional connection and where I thought I could do the most good.

And in the middle of it all was St. Jude Children's Research Hospital.

A friend of mine, Rhubarb Jones, went to Jacksonville State at the same time as I did and later became a legendary country DJ, a genuine Hall of Famer. He had a morning show in Atlanta and was working to raise money for St. Jude. He wanted me to meet Danny Thomas, the founder and driving force behind St. Jude, and see for myself how impressive he was. Before long I was hopping into the private Alabama plane at four in the morning to fly over to Atlanta to appear on his show and add my name to the cause.

I continued to have contact with Danny, and the more I saw of him, the more my respect for him grew. His passion for the kids at St. Jude was infectious, and I quickly became infected. This was something I felt strongly in my heart. It was, pardon the cliché, a no-brainer.

Danny Thomas was a TV star and show-business entrepreneur best known for his hit network sitcom *Make Room for Daddy* (later renamed *The Danny Thomas Show*) in the 1950s and '60s. Danny founded St. Jude Children's Research Hospital in 1962 on the idea that "no child should die in the dawn of life." St. Jude takes care of some of the sickest kids in the world, and it does it almost entirely through donations. Seventy-five percent of its funding comes through their fund-raising wing, called the American Lebanese Syrian Associated Charities (ALSAC), also created by Danny Thomas. Kids with leukemia, sickle cell anemia, and other catastrophic pediatric diseases come to Memphis to receive some of the most advanced care available. In 1996 the head of the Department of Immunology at St. Jude, Dr. Peter Doherty, shared the Nobel Prize in Physiology or Medicine for his work with the immune system.

And the kids come there for free.

St. Jude is an enormous operation. When he started it, Danny Thomas promised four things: (1) world-class patient care, (2) a special emphasis on scientific research into the causes and cures of these terrible childhood diseases, (3) the free sharing of this research, and (4)—perhaps most important—no child would ever be denied care because of race, religion, country of origin, or a family's inability to pay.

Because of this commitment to every sick child, the hospital normally pays all expenses of the uninsured and all expenses of the insured beyond what their insurance pays, beginning with the transportation of both the patient and parents to Memphis. It pays for the lodgings of loved ones, their food, and all ancillary patient costs beyond the direct care of a particular illness, including psychiatric services, if needed, or optometry or dentistry. St. Jude has brought kids from all over the United States and from seventy countries to their facility and in doing so has made great strides in increasing the survival rates of millions of children with devastating diseases. For instance, the rate of recovery from acute lymphoblastic leukemia, the most prevalent form of childhood cancer, has increased from only 4 percent in 1962 to 94 percent today. That's Danny Thomas's legacy.

I like to call St. Jude "The Miracle on Beale Street," Beale being the legendary Memphis street where blues greats like Louis Armstrong and B.B. King cut their musical teeth.

All of this work at St. Jude comes with a steep price tag, of course. The financial cost for one day of operation at St. Jude is almost $1.3 million. And most of it comes from people like you and me. Last year they raised $592 million through 30,000 fund-raising events around the country. The average contribution was $25.09.

I got a lot of my education about St. Jude from a man named John Moses, former CEO of ALSAC, and from Dick Shadyac. John is from Wilkes-Barre, Pennsylvania. An attorney by trade, he got hooked on St. Jude upon meeting Danny Thomas for thirty seconds as a sixteen-year-old boy. I met John in the late '80s at a St. Jude annual meeting. The organization had become enormously diverse since the hospital opened in 1962 and was as multicultural in its fund-raising as in its admission policy.

John likes to tell a story about me that underscores our friendship and in my mind is both flattering and embarrassing. In any case, here's what happened:

John had never seen Alabama in concert, so I invited him and his wife to the York County Fair in York, Pennsylvania, to see us perform before seven thousand energetic fans. I had invited him backstage after the show, but he and his wife started to leave, thinking I'd be too tired or inundated with fans to talk to them. I'll let John tell the rest: "As we were walking out, the PA system announced, 'Attorney John Moses, please come to the stage area.' So we did as told, went through a security check with fifty other people waiting to see Randy, and headed backstage. We found ourselves in a basement of some sort, with green-colored concrete floors that were old and cracking. Randy met with each and every person, signed an autograph, took a picture, and chatted. I was at the very back of the line, and the crowd was pretty much gone. The woman directly in front of me, probably in her forties, was in a wheelchair and had trouble speaking. When it was her turn, Randy took a picture with her, signed something, and then asked, 'Now, is there anything else I can do for you?'

"She looked up at him and in her very hard-to-understand speech said, 'Yes. I want you to sing "Angels Among Us" with me.'

"So Randy, without skipping a beat, knelt down on that cold concrete floor and held her hand as the two of them sang 'Angels Among Us' from start to finish. There was no photography, no press, no television, no nothing. He was singing the song both with her and for her.

"And I have got to tell you, that was one of the most moving moments of my entire life, and believe me, I have been exposed to a lot of heart-touching moments after decades of working with St. Jude. And I will never, ever forget that image. The two of them, Randy kneeling on this cold cement floor, singing."

I remember that moment well, and I also remember the endless hours and meetings and red-eye flights and budget sessions and black-tie affairs that John has coordinated to raise the money to keep St. Jude operating. On any given weekend, there are fifty or more events going on around the country to raise money for St. Jude, and John is in charge of every one of them. He probably knows all five and a half million base donors by name.

I like John's story because it underscores how that song, "Angels Among Us," became such a big part of the Alabama legacy. The song, written by Becky Hobbs and Don Goodman, arrived after we had just experienced a local tragedy. One of Alison's high-school basketball teammates had been killed in a car crash after a big game. Randa was only two at the time and peppered me with questions about where this girl was now and why she wasn't playing basketball anymore and why God had done this to her. She just wanted answers to the questions we all ask. I wanted so much to be able to answer her in a song but didn't have that song in my head.

Then Becky and Don's song arrived. Becky had had an experience many years before when a mysterious male voice, perhaps her guardian angel, had told her to be very careful, and soon after while on the road, that warning prevented her whole band from being killed by an 18-wheeler. I heard the song and connected it to the girl who died in the crash. As Randa understood, she was now one of the angels among us. So one day while we were sitting on the couch, Randa asked me to tell her the words to the song again, and I began to speak them to her before I began to sing them. As I recited them, Randa's little arm got tighter and tighter around my neck. That's when I knew how I would record the song and sing it onstage.

The song was not initially a popular choice for the band or for the label to add to one of our records. It was not a typical Alabama song, that's for sure. It is partially spoken and has a children's chorus in the background. It is also overtly spiritual and inspirational, not an Alabama trademark. But despite the misgivings, we recorded it, and it struck a deep chord with millions of fans like the woman backstage at the York County Fair. I can't tell you the number of copies sold to date, but if it isn't our most popular song, it's pretty close.

We released "Angels Among Us" in 1994 on the *Cheap Seats* album, and it only made it to No. 28 on the U.S. Country Chart and No. 122 on the U.S. Hot 100 Pop Chart, though it stayed on the Top Singles sales chart for over a year. Since we first put it out, it has become an anthem of hope for many people and a standard at high-school concerts, benefit functions, and funerals. It's a song I often use in conjunction with charities like St. Jude. Danny Thomas was clearly "an angel among us" who has given thousands of kids another chance in life.

I personally felt an appreciation for the song because it seems to mirror in its lyrics much of the feeling I have always had about the guiding hand of God in my life. I have felt that divine assistance in everything from that early childhood attack of hepatitis, which the prayers of my relatives helped me survive, to all the potential tragedies and missteps I have been able to avoid up to today—including weathering my emotional downturn without destroying all that we had worked to build.

Part of the song says: "When life held troubled times, and had me down on my knees, there's always been someone there to come along and comfort me." How would I have survived the crises of my life without the love and support of Kelly and the kids? Thank God, these particular angels were there.

From the first time I met Danny Thomas, I understood the enormous good St. Jude does and the enormous need for funds for them to do it. I stayed involved in St. Jude activities through the '80s, and as I saw Danny Thomas start to get on in years and his health failing, I felt in my heart that I had to somehow do more. In 1989 Danny was asked to be the keynote speaker at the Country Radio Seminar in Nashville. For health reasons, he couldn't make it, so the St. Jude people asked me to fill in. I wasn't a professional speaker or anything, but I knew this was something I cared about and could talk from the heart about. Facing all those country-radio programmers and executives from all over the country, I had the perfect opportunity to challenge them to help continue Danny's dream.

From this impulse was born the idea for Country Cares, which we got off the ground in the late '80s and which, almost twenty years later, I still consider one of the main priorities in my life.

Country Cares began as a radiothon among national country-music stations to raise money for the hospital. The first year, we used a single DJ in Memphis who then syndicated his appeal to other stations in other markets. It was not a roaring success. In fact John remembers that at the first meeting where he and I met, there was serious talk of scrapping the whole idea. One staffer got up and pleaded that the program continue because the potential was certainly there. Fortunately I realized why it wasn't working and what we could do to fix it.

We completely changed the format of the radiothon. We made it a local event at each participating station, involving a local radio personality the local audience knew and listened to. The station could run the radiothon over a one- or two-day period whenever they wanted to in the course of the year, and we would supply all the supporting material to make the event both urgent and exciting.

Say the local Minneapolis country station, one of our biggest supporters, cancels all their regular programming for one day to run the Country Cares radiothon for St. Jude. They would play a song by, say, Sarah Evans or Keith Urban, then Sarah or Keith would come on with a direct pitch, followed by testimonies of parents and kids at St. Jude or overview information about the hospital's mission. If you responded to our call for action, you might come down to the mall where the program was being broadcast that day and pick up an autographed Keith Urban T-shirt in return for a hefty donation. Or you could call a phone bank and make a donation, hopefully one as a "partner in hope," which was a commitment of $20 a month.

In the end, everybody profits. We have periodic gatherings where radio people come in to meet the stars. The stars do a good deed and make more contacts with the people who play their songs. And they are all there, slapping backs and exchanging phone numbers, in the service of a bunch of very sick kids in a hospital in Memphis.

Today we have 204 country stations nationwide involved in Country Cares on an annual basis. Teri Watson, a former music director from Los Angeles, is in charge of all Country Care activities full-time. The program has worked better than our wildest dreams. Every city and station has its own method, employing local companies, local advertisers, and local citizens. So far in 2008, Minneapolis holds the record—they've raised $2.1 million alone. The most money every raised in San Francisco was the year they had the earthquake. It's a miracle how much people care.

Since its inception in its current form in 1989, Country Cares has raised $344.5 million, according to John Moses. There is also now a sister enterprise called Radio Cares involving forty-five noncountry stations and a similar effort in the Hispanic radio market that has raised almost $20 million.

To keep this giant ship afloat takes some effort. When needed, I'm on the phone with radio programmers, DJs, and friends in the music business whom we need to make promotional tapes and personal appearances and visits to St. Jude to tape kids and parents and doctors.

Kelly sees all of this going on from her unique, supportive perspective. She's there when I have to get up from the middle of dinner because some station in California needs me to come on live and talk to their listeners about why this is so important to me. Kelly says it best: "It really doesn't matter if he and I are passionately taking a bath together or working on a fence post or visiting a sick cow. If it's that time for him to call at 6:45 in the morning or 10:45 at night, Randy stops what he's doing and makes the call."

Probably the greatest pleasure for me involving St. Jude and Country Cares is the opportunity to visit with patients and parents at the hospital. When I'm there, I make an effort to visit every room I can, talk to the kid stuck in that hospital bed, and learn a little more about how he or she is dealing with such an awful situation. And lots of times, kids from Country Cares will show up at an Alabama concert, like the time the audience lights went on and I could read on the back of a little girl's T-shirt the words I'm Living Proof Country Cares. She was a cancer survivor, and when she came up onstage and told us that, I was blown away. If music is sustenance for my soul, this kind of work is definitely sustenance for my heart.

And much like at the June Jam, the lineup of artists who have taken the time to participate in the radio effort or come to the hospital to visit kids and maybe sung them their own versions of "Angels Among Us" is lengthy: Kenny Chesney, John Michael

Montgomery, Martina McBride, Lonestar, Jewel, Carrie Under-
wood, Keith Urban, and Vince Gill and Amy Grant. There are just
too many to keep track of. Oh, did I mention Marlo and Tony
Thomas, who have taken the reins from their dad and helped
keep his dream alive? It's a long list, believe me.

In 1997, ALSAC held a gala in Memphis to celebrate the fifti-
eth anniversary of St. Jude and honor the man who started it all.
Before over a thousand people, it was my very great honor when
Tony Thomas, Danny's son, presented me with the Founder's
Award because of Country Cares. My whole family was there to
witness this, not to mention to hear Tony Bennett sing and Phil
Donahue, husband of Marlo Thomas, tell jokes. It was a very
special evening.

I'll give John Moses the last word on the subject of St. Jude:
"I think Randy is one of the people he sings about when he sings
'Angels Among Us.' I think he was sent by someone up above—as
the lyrics say—'to teach us how to live, to show us how to give,
and to guide us in the light of love.'"

Gratifying words, John, and certainly words that could easily
apply to you and the millions of people supporting the vital work
of St. Jude.

I don't spend all my free time working with St. Jude. I have many
other passions that get me out of bed in the morning and put
me in touch with the community at large, especially if it involves
helping farmers and preserving the family farm. I'll never forget

the time we performed for Willie Nelson's inaugural Farm Aid benefit concert at the University of Illinois in Champaign on September 22, 1985. Now a twenty-three-year institution, the first Farm Aid was a seminal event in raising national awareness about the plight of thousands of family farmers, and we were proud to be there alongside Johnny Cash, Charlie Daniels, Bob Dylan, and a dozen other major artists.

What has forever stayed with me from that day is a hand-written letter I read on national television from a woman named Sue Massey of Hollandale, Wisconsin. The Massey family—Sue, her husband, Kenny, and their five children—was about to lose its dairy-farm-turned-egg-farm to foreclosure, a common story among family farmers in those times. Sue's words struck a chord with every person in that crowd in Champaign: "My husband, Kenny, is a third-generation farmer, but we are faced with an approaching forced farm sale. Words can't relate how destructive this can be. One's self-esteem drops to rock bottom, and feel-ings of failure move in. The stress can be hard on a marriage and devastating to the kids.

"In 1968 the farm was debt free. . . . Then suddenly prices dropped drastically and stayed down way too long. . . . Now all that's left are the bills. . . . Farmers aren't looking to get rich. It's the simple things they love and understand. . . . Raising crops and watching the children grow . . . being close, being together with the family as fruits of our labor. . . .

"This is a plea for help from our young family in its struggle to hang on. Please forgive us for asking, but we are at the point of desperation. The forced sale is within 8 to 12 weeks and time is of the essence . . ."

There was really nothing we could do to save their farm—after a four-year struggle to hold on to it, they finally gave it up. The farm that had been in Kenny's family for more than eighty years was sold at auction on the steps of the courthouse in Dodgeville, Wisconsin. The Masseys went on to find a new life for themselves. We couldn't work a miracle at Farm Aid, but we put a human face and a family name to the plight of struggling farmers everywhere, to praise their efforts to fight to the very end, even as they failed.

The story of the Massey family and their deep love of farming and the land simply reaffirmed my commitment to devote as much time as possible in helping rural kids get off to a good start in the agricultural and cattle businesses. I was raised on a farm, I still live and work on a farm, and I think farming is vital to our economy and is a healthy, productive way of life. As I've said before, it'll be a sad day in America if and when we become as dependent on foreign food and fiber sources as we are on foreign energy sources today.

My goal is to encourage young people to stay in the field of farming. One of my efforts has been to lobby the legislature of the state of Alabama to actively promote family farming as a career choice. To this end, I helped create a $50,000 annual scholarship fund that would be awarded to kids who participate in state livestock competitions and show lambs, goats, steers, and the like. The recipients would receive scholarship money for college, but not necessarily as agriculture majors. Unfortunately, given the shifting winds of state politics, the program has since been shuttled for other priorities.

Farming has an increasingly bad image in this hi-tech age. I walk into a classroom in Alabama, or anywhere probably, and the majority of kids and teachers kind of look at you funny when you start talking about the joys of growing food or raising cattle. You even mention planting corn or picking cotton, and they smirk.

At this point I usually look at them and ask, "So, what are you going to do when no one you know can raise potatoes or run a milking operation? What are you going to do when someone in a foreign country sets the price and the availability of your most basic foodstuffs? Are you going to eat that computer you have in your hands? Are you going to milk that iPod?"

In the long run, family farming is a way of maintaining control over our lives, to be independent and self-sustaining. In the short run, it is a great way to teach youngsters the value of dedication and hard work. Because of my work with programs like the scholarship fund that took me all over the state, I've met a lot of kids who are enthusiastic about rural life. For the most part, no matter their circumstances or backgrounds, they are courteous, respectful of others, self-starting, and hardworking. I heard one judge in a livestock competition sum it up nicely. He said, "I want you kids to look around at all of you who are showing today. Because, believe it or not, you're probably looking at your future governor, or future senator, or the guy or gal who will be running the factory you'll be working in. If you go back and check the backgrounds of many of our social leaders, you'll see that many were raised in the country and participated in events just like this."

I know this firsthand. I have a daughter who loves living on a farm and working with livestock and is also the salutatorian of her high-school class and played Lydia the Gypsy in the student production of *Hansel and Gretel*. (Her sister, Alison, also starred in a number of school productions and was valedictorian.) There is no contradiction between being a well-rounded, educated person and getting your hands dirty.

Among my duties in this area, I am the chairman of youth efforts at the Alabama State Junior Heifer and Steer Show, held annually in Montgomery. I helped start the rookie divisions, five or six in number, areas where kids who have never shown before get a chance at some recognition. We came up with this inexpensive medallion to give to all the competitors, no matter where they place. The truth is, kids who have never been in an event like this most likely will do a poor job of showing animals they have raised. But they get a chance to be judged fairly and encouraged to come back next year in better shape.

Whenever I'm with these first-timers, I remember how shy and withdrawn I was when I was their age. Like me, they may go to school and sit in the corner, and no one pays any attention to them. They may feel self-conscious because they're from the country, don't have much money, or even have cotton dust on their hands. But at the show there is this one brief moment when a judge, probably from Auburn or some other august institution, is looking at them and taking both them or their work seriously. They are the center of attention, and, win or lose, they can't help but feel good about it. The next year, those kids won't be the rookies at the show. Their moments with the judge could affect their whole lives.

Sometimes they're a little confused but still as straight and honest as they come. One judge told me about a brief conversation he had with a very young competitor with a pained look on her face.

"So, young lady," he said, admiring her entry, "what do you think about your heifer?"

"Right now," she said, "I don't like her much."

"Why not?" he asked.

"Well," she said, "because she's stepping on my toes."

A memorable encounter with one young farmer-to-be has stayed with me since the day I met him. I was walking through the aisles of the show, and this kid, probably about twelve years old, walks up to me boldly and sticks out his hand. I shake it and ask him how he's doing. He says, "I'm doing fine, sir. I'm from Crenshaw County. The only people in my 4-H Club are me and my sisters and brothers."

Impressed, I couldn't wait to see how he did in the competition. I watch as he and his brother walk into the showring and show a cow and a calf. And they finish dead last! Upon the announcement, both my friend from Crenshaw County and his little brother walk over to the judge, shake his hand, and walk out of the ring with their heads held high. It was very classy.

And I thought, *Watch out for those two.*

I meet a lot of genuinely good kids like this who only want a chance to excel in an area they know and love. Some come from divorced families where one parent moves away and they lose the support they need to prepare a new animal for the show. We then try to find volunteers who can help that kid break a steer and keep competing. We don't want to lose that kid.

Many of the great farmers in Alabama, I've come to learn through this work, are African Americans, long marginalized by prejudice and inability to get the support of lending officers at the banks, people who can determine the life or death of a family farm. Now, at our statewide steer show, the proportion of black kids participating is ever increasing, great news for farming in Alabama. These kids will be successful—they'll put their talent with animals on display and learn and grow—and I think any parents, teachers, or coaches, no matter how they might smirk at the future of farming, would see this if they came to a show.

As you no doubt have gathered, I have very strong feelings about this. I feel it is critical, especially for the state of Alabama, that we stand up for these kids. Whatever it takes, we need to keep them on the farm and get the farm strong and prosperous. Having gained so much from growing up in the country, from the music I make to the Herefords and Angus I raise, I think it would be criminal to see Alabama farmland turned into subdivisions and shopping malls. Even up here on this relatively isolated mountain, I can feel the houses getting closer and closer. The farms need to be left alone.

If there's not a future in farming, you might say, then we ain't got a future.

I have met many fine people outside of music since Alabama first began to perform, from John Moses to that twelve-year-old future farmer who was perfectly happy to come in last at the Heifer and Steer Show, but a man whose name I must add to this chronicle is my late, dear friend Dale Earnhardt. Dale and I had careers that almost perfectly paralleled each other's. We both got going around 1980 and grew from there. I think we were alike personally as well, both of us being quiet and introspective when we were performing for the public. When Kelly said that "it's hard to hide real people," I think she must have had Dale in mind. He was one of the most real I ever knew.

Ever since I listened to races on the radio with my daddy, I have always loved NASCAR. At one point, long before NASCAR was a major sport on TV, I tried to get racing and TV together. I hosted a TNN show and invited a bunch of greats like Bill Elliott and Sterling Marlin to appear, as well as the great Bobby Allison, after his career-ending accident at the Pocono Raceway in 1988. My first question to him was, "So, Bobby, what was the highlight of your career?" He said, "I can't remember." He couldn't remember because that wreck had wiped out his memory. I had just asked a really stupid question.

I met Dale Earnhardt for the first time in 1981 when neither of us was all that well known. He had been NASCAR Rookie of the Year in 1979 and won the Winston Cup Championship in 1980, about the same time Alabama was starting its string of twenty-one straight hits. A friend of mine named Ralph Seagraves, who liked to refer to himself as "just a little old cigarette salesman from Winston-Salem, North Carolina" but was in fact the man who created the NASCAR Winston Cup, called one day to say he had someone he wanted me to meet. Ralph had always helped out Alabama charities whenever he could. I called Kelly, who was shopping down at the grocery store at the time, and she rushed home in time to meet Ralph and his guests—Dale and Teresa Earnhardt.

We had just moved out of the little brown house and into our big house across the road. I remember Dale's saying, "Man, I love this house." Then he sat down on the hearth of the fireplace and said, "You know, I hope I can build my wife a house like this someday." And this was *after* he'd won his first NASCAR Championship. He never took his success for granted, which is why he worked so hard and was one of the most hard-charging drivers in the sport, if not *the* most, until the day he died at Daytona. He was the kind of driver my daddy always liked to cheer on while listening to races on the radio, and when I went to a race at places like Talladega or Charlotte, it was basically to see Dale.

I'd see him whenever both of our insane schedules allowed— he came to the Alabama employee-and-friends Christmas Party one year—and in 2000 he invited Kelly and me to his big New Year's party in North Carolina. It was the millennium New Year's, the craziest one of them all. I said, "Dale, you know, they're telling me stuff like all the clocks are going to stop, all the computers are

223

going to mess up, it's going to be Armageddon, the end of times, plus, I don't really like to fly." I was completely exhausted at the time and planned to sleep in my own bed on New Year's.

He wouldn't give up. I tried another tack, completely true, in fact. "You know, Dale, I don't know what kind of parties you throw, but when Kelly and I go to a party, we don't drink and act crazy, so it might not be a lot of fun for us." He said, "I guarantee you this is not going to be like that." So we went.

He was exactly right. It wasn't a wild and crazy millennium party. It turned out to be one of the happiest, most relaxed times he and I ever spent together. The next morning, he got me up early, and we went for a long drive on his farm, looking at the deer and just talking about our lives. Dale was like I am today. He cared more about raising deer and other wildlife and admiring them than shooting them. Kelly and I ended up staying a couple of days in his place, spending the kind of time together we never could at a racetrack. At a race, the minute Dale walked out of his trailer, he belonged to everybody, friends and strangers alike.

I'm so eternally grateful that I spent that holiday with him. It was the last time, it turned out, that I would see him alive.

On the Saturday before the Sunday of the 2001 Daytona 500, our son, Heath, then in college, had a baseball game we were looking forward to. Given my road schedule while my kids were growing up, if I could figure a way to go to one of their sports events or plays or livestock shows, I wouldn't miss it. Kelly had never been to a Daytona 500. We were all ready to go until Heath's Saturday varsity baseball game at Samford University got rained out and postponed until the next day, the day of the race. So we made the decision not to go to Daytona. We wanted to watch our boy play ball.

I had the radio to listen to the race, and early on Dale was running second or third and seemed to be in great shape. So I said to myself, *Well, he's running good,* and I shut it off when the game got going. The game lasted awhile, and so when I finally got back to the car, I called our bus driver, Jeff Rucks, because I knew both he and his daddy loved Dale and he'd tell me how the race went. When I got him, he just started crying. He said, "Man, we lost Dale." I said, "What do you mean, 'we lost Dale'?" He then told me the whole story of the crash on the last lap of the race that had killed Dale. Kelly and I both burst into tears. It was such a shocking, unbelievable loss.

In a way, I'm happy that I wasn't there that day, that fate had made it so we were with Heath instead. I wouldn't want to keep on seeing that crash in my mind. I wouldn't want that to be my last memory of Dale. I'd much rather remember the time we had together at New Year's when I think of him. I'd much rather remember the guy who loved to hunt and fish and simply be outdoors, not The Intimidator, but the reserved, soft-spoken friend of mine.

Teresa called Kelly a day or two later and asked me to sing at Dale's service. So Kelly and I went back to North Carolina, and I sang at the private family service. The same day, I sang again at the big public service. That day was one of the most gut-wrenching days I've ever experienced. I don't really know how I got through it.

I sang two songs: "Angels Among Us" and the song I had written for Kelly almost thirty years earlier when she was leaving South Carolina to go join her dad in Germany: "Goodbye," otherwise known as "Kelly's Song."

> *That one word hurts so bad*
> *When you lose the best you've had*
> *But you keep the faith and pray to return . . .*

Sometime after the service, some of the record people said, "You know, if we release those two songs sung live like that, we could probably sell six or seven million copies. That's what happened when Elton John's people released 'Candle in the Wind' after the death of Lady Di." I said, "No, I don't care if we'd sell a hundred million, I'm not going to make money off of my friend." And that was that.

I don't think that if Dale had survived that terrible day at Daytona, he would have continued to race full-time for too many more years. Something I always respected about him was his love and devotion to his wife—in the face of all the temptations and distractions of his celebrated life—and I think he could see the day when racing would take a backseat to spending more of his life with her. Remember, I said that our lives in many ways paralleled each other's. About the time Dale died was the time when I and the rest of Alabama were thinking about making a critical transition in our lives and the life of the group.

We had reached the twenty-fifth year of an amazing musical journey, our silver anniversary. It was time for what came to be known as Alabama's "American Farewell Tour."

226

# CHAPTER 10

# THE FAREWELL TOUR

*I wish we could've played one more*
*We hope you remember*
*We're just the boys in the band*
*And what keeps the fires a burnin'*
*Is always, you, the fans.*

**"THE FANS" BY RANDY OWEN, TEDDY GENTRY,**
**AND GREG FOWLER**

As the new century began, none of us—Teddy, Jeff, or I—had the thought that it was time for Alabama to hang it up because we were over the hill or had worn out our welcome. None of us felt our time was up, nor did Dale Morris or RCA or all the people who supported Alabama. We had enough hits under our belt, and the ability to generate more, that we could have gone on touring for years to come. In fact, at a long three-plus-hours Alabama concert, we could perform a whole playlist of nothing but No. 1

hit songs, one after another, and still have a bunch left over. Plus, there were timeless non–No. 1 songs we love to do, like "Angels Among Us" or "Dancin', Shaggin' on the Boulevard" or "Tar Top" or . . . you get the point.

When we were touring in 2000 and 2001, we could look out at the audience and see two or three generations of people staring back at us. The kids who used to wear the Lynyrd Skynyrd T-shirts when their parents brought them to a concert in the early '80s were now sitting next to *their* kids wearing Coldplay T-shirts. And the women who got chills during a performance of "Feels So Right" in 1994 were still turning and smiling at their husbands. We were still packing them in.

Professional musicians are a lot like professional boxers or athletes of any kind—they never know quite when to step away. I'm a fan of Roger Clemens, who formally retired from baseball, then kept coming back for four more seasons. Muhammad Ali probably went back for one too many fights. It's a tough call. I'm also a huge Packer and Brett Favre fan, and I sure respect his wanting to play, now with the Jets.

For Alabama, by 2002 we had reached a point of decision about how to carry on what by then had been a twenty-two-year tradition as a recording group and a good seven or eight years before that as Myrtle Beach's own Wildcountry. We had done enough and gathered enough memorabilia to fill up a fair-sized Alabama Fan Club and Museum in downtown Fort Payne, open three days a week. We could have easily gone on touring, maybe forever for all we knew, but what we did know was how we *didn't* want to end up. We didn't want to keep going until the luster and distinction had completely worn off the name Alabama. We didn't want to become a nostalgia band or end up playing smaller and smaller rooms in Las Vegas or Branson. We'd already done our stint, a long one, as a bar band. We didn't want to end up a high-class bar band in a bigger, glitzier version of Myrtle Beach.

Personally, I wasn't quite sure what to do at that point. After decades of continual touring, my instinct was just to stop for a while and let the next move come about in some organic way. I wanted to take a year off and see what would happen. I felt I had lost the focus I had always had when it came to music, and I wanted to get that back. Other members of the group had their own ideas about what to do next, but I thought stepping away was the right way for me to gain a new purpose and passion.

Kelly and I had many long talks about exactly what to do. She kept reminding me what a big transition was coming up no matter what we did. It was a little like jumping off a cliff. That's why I kept thinking about a sabbatical instead of a clean break. After structuring almost my entire adulthood around being on the road, giving that up was frankly a bit frightening. I could sense the relief in not thinking about Alabama every minute of the day, but I could also sense the loss. Family aside, Alabama was my life and my identity. It was not something I could just casually let go of.

Like most things to do with Alabama, the Farewell Tour evolved as the right way to end one phase of our career and enter the next one. Dale puts it another way: "It happened because I talked them into it," which is true. We didn't want to break up as a group—we didn't break up as a group and haven't broken up as a group to this day. I can't tell you how many times I've had to explain that to reporters. The idea of a big farewell tour was simply a way of focusing on our accomplishments to that point, giving our fans a chance to see us at the very top of our game, playing our best songs, surrounded by the best production possible, and walking away from touring as champions, not as people who had stayed too long at the party. We wanted to bow out with style, grace, and enough raw energy to still blow the roof off the house.

Again, by doing a farewell tour, we were forging new ground in country music. Country fans, as had been said to the point that it's a cliché by now, are the most loyal fans on the planet. You win over a country fan, you've generally got a fan for life. For this reason, country acts tend to keep going until they expire onstage. I mean, who wouldn't want to see Merle Haggard or George Jones in person, no matter how old they are? They are timeless songwriters and performers. A "farewell tour" is a tradition among rock and pop groups, except for the Rolling Stones, of course. Think of The Band's farewell concert, The Last Waltz. Think of Cher's Last Tour, in 2002, after forty years in the business. The Judds had done a final tour in the early '90s when Naomi Judd was diagnosed with hepatitis, but that was an exception. In the same way country record labels in 1980 said, "Sorry, we don't sign bands," a lot of people in the business in 2002 said, "What? You can't have a farewell tour! You're still big stars!"

We announced the Alabama American Farewell Tour during the May 2002 telecast of the Academy of Country Music Awards and announced it to none other than our great friend ACM producer Dick Clark. It was a bittersweet moment. Sure, I'd finally have time to spend with my wife after almost thirty years of a marriage where the music always came first, and a major burden was about to be lifted off of my shoulders, but at the same time, an era of my life was ending and certainly in terms of musical accomplishment, the best years of my life.

Enlisting the help and guidance of Marc Oswald as well as Dale, Barbara, Greg, and our merry band of stone pros, we spent almost two years planning this massive tour. Initially the plan was to do forty cities in 2003 and call it a day. After we did the first forty, we realized we weren't quite through, given the enormous response we had received, so we scheduled another forty shows that took us through 2004. In all it was a four-year operation from start to finish, and it brought all the satisfaction and sense of completion that we all hoped it would. It was a kick-ass way to say both thanks and goodbye.

The first forty-show leg of the Farewell Tour—lasting most of 2003—took us to large-scale venues in major cities like Atlanta, Chicago, and Washington, DC. There are so many highlights of that year that I don't really know where to begin. Probably the single most moving event of the whole year took place in Washington in August. With the help of the Veterans Administration and a lot of other fine people connected to the military, we scheduled a special performance at Nissan Pavilion in nearby Bristow,

Virginia, to honor all the soldiers fighting on the two battlefronts of Iraq and Afghanistan.

We had long done events to salute our military, such as performing with Bob Hope a number of times, the most memorable to me being a patriotic event at Constitution Hall in Washington. What has always stayed with me was a trip we made afterward to the National Vietnam Veterans Memorial, "The Wall." It was snowing that day, and Mr. Hope was quite old, but he nevertheless got out of his car and walked right up to the wall to pay his respects. When I mentioned how much I admired him for doing that, he gave me a sage piece of advice. He said, "Listen, if you are going to err, err on the side of your country."

On every stop of the Farewell Tour, we paid special tribute to the troops and often brought soldiers in the audience onstage to be recognized for their service. After all, Kelly was an army brat, and we've always been close to people who devote their lives to, and sometimes give their lives for, our country. Kelly enlisted Mack Cooper and Danny Mack Hughes to ship free socks to the troops overseas, courtesy of UPS. At one point we sent a batch of socks directly to her brother, Col. Jason Pyle, then serving in Iraq. It was great to hear directly from Jason what those socks meant to his comrades over there. As I write this, Jason has just returned from his second tour of duty in Iraq. He has also served in Afghanistan. His service brings those wars, and all the men and women fighting them, very close to home.

In any case, the event at the Nissan Pavilion was the culmi-
nation of our longtime support of American soldiers, at least in
terms of Alabama on tour.

It was actually just one part of two incredible days interacting
with the military. At the concert itself, we set reduced prices for
all military families and then bussed in several busloads of injured soldiers from the National Naval Medical Center in Bethesda,
Maryland, and the Walter Reed Army Medical Center in Silver
Spring, Maryland. As part of the show, we invited twenty to thirty
"wounded warriors," as the military rightfully calls them, onstage
where they introduced themselves individually, along with hometowns, and told where they had fought. As they stood beside us,
we performed and I sang "America the Beautiful," which is Kelly's
very favorite patriotic song. It was an indescribable moment.

That same night we were given two very special awards
for our ongoing efforts to support the men and women in
uniform—the USO Rising Star Award and the Pentagon 9/11
Medallion.

The next day we were again honored by being asked to lay
a wreath at the Tomb of the Unknowns at Arlington National
Cemetery. I had personally done this once before a few years
back, but in the wake of 9/11 and the two wars going on at the
time, this ceremony took on even more urgency and meaning.
The Tomb Guards, who wear no insignia of rank, patrol the tomb
twenty-four hours a day, seven days a week. It was just an honor
to get to meet and talk to them.

Finally, I visited both Bethesda and Walter Reed that day and talked at length with other injured soldiers just returning from the front. It's hard to put into words the impact of this sequence of events. Greg Fowler has said that "the whole days, to me, personally, were the two finest days I've ever spent as part of Alabama." I'd have to concur.

Because of the wartime circumstances, we started getting requests from soldiers who were about to leave the country to come onstage and publicly propose marriage to their sweethearts. Word must have gotten around, because this started happening at every show, sometimes two or three times. By the end of the tour we were batting 100 percent—not one of them got turned down in front of thousands of witnesses.

Another special moment of that first part of the Farewell Tour happened in June of 2003. Teresa Earnhardt, Dale's widow, was trying to figure out some way to pay tribute to Dale and raise money for the Dale Earnhardt Foundation. One of the major projects of the foundation was the Dale Earnhardt Legacy Forest, a direct outgrowth of his love of the outdoors. Teresa and I came up with the idea of a daylong music festival to take place right on the grounds of the Daytona International Speedway, the site of his death. No one had ever used the speedway for this purpose— a big music show—and we figured if there were ever an occasion to break with tradition and use the place for a nonracing event, this was it. The speedway people agreed, and so did a whole number of major country and rock stars who interrupted their summer tours to join us, including Brooks and Dunn, Kenny Chesney, and Sheryl Crow.

The event dovetailed nicely into the Farewell Tour, in that we were all saying farewell to Dale in a positive public way. Logistically, on the other hand, it was a nightmare. We had long before booked Farewell Tour stops in Nashville and Birmingham for the exact same weekend as the Daytona concert, but the Daytona date was the only one available in the middle of racing season to allow drivers like Dale Jr. to attend. On that Friday night, we played Nashville. The next morning we hopped a plane to Daytona. That afternoon we played the Dale show, and as soon as the last note was hit, we caught a van to the airport as a major thunderstorm gathered overhead, flew to Birmingham, got a police escort to the hall, and walked directly onstage and starting playing. My mama would have said we only made it because of God's hand, and she would probably be right.

Because the Farewell Tour was a one-time-only, never-to-happen-again event, we created a special ticket package—only a hundred tickets available per show—that involved a front-row seat, a signed photo with the whole group, and a special limited-edition Les Paul Jr. "Alabama" electric guitar, autographed by the whole crew. In general and as always, though, we tried to keep both tickets and merchandise within a reasonable price range for our fans. We just figured that you shouldn't have to get a loan from the bank to bring your family to the concert. There was sometimes a problem with pricing of merchandise at Alabama shows. Years ago, local concessions contractors would want to step in as middlemen and jack up prices to line their pockets. When we saw this coming, we simply withdrew our merchandise from the venue. This didn't make the local operators too happy. In fact, one night Greg Fowler was onstage in Hartford, Connecticut, explaining this situation to the audience, when the venue people got so mad they just pulled the plug on all the power. We didn't really care. We were there for the fans, not the promoters.

The Farewell Tour, as originally conceived, officially ended at Rosemont Stadium, or Allstate Arena, in Chicago at the end of 2003. But we weren't through yet. Because of the ticket demand, we decided to do one last forty-show tour in 2004 that would hit many of the smaller venues missed in the first go-around. In early 2004, right before we began to tune up for this tour, I was hit with another health crisis. This time it wasn't something that had anything to do with a possible heart ailment. This time it hit me in the head—vertigo.

And like the attack in 1992, this one happened at home. We were just about to take off for San Antonio, Texas, and the San Antonio Rodeo and Livestock Show. We were also about to receive the 2004 Country Radio Broadcasters Career Achievement Award. I was at home on the floor exercising, stretching my neck, that kind of thing. And then, all of a sudden, the whole world starting spinning around at a breakneck speed. It was shocking and frightening. It was as close to an out-of-body experience as I've ever had. I genuinely thought I was going to die or maybe even had already died.

Kelly, working out right next to me, jumped when she heard me holler as the world around me was spinning out of control, and her first thought was that I was having a heart attack. She could see that I was pale and my eyes were darting back and forth. When I described the spinning, she immediately said, "You're having vertigo." She would certainly know. In the early 1990s, she was diagnosed with inner-ear trouble and occasionally has vertigo-like symptoms. Later I found out that Dale Morris had also suffered from recurring episodes of vertigo. Like anxiety and depression, it is often something people just live with instead of going for help.

Kelly got me on the bed and gave me some of the medication, called meclizine, that she had been prescribed for her inner-ear disturbance. It is a highly concentrated antihistamine that will dry up any fluid that's in your eardrum. People often take it while flying to combat altitude sickness. It seemed to do the trick, at least temporarily.

It took me awhile to even stand up, but the episode soon passed. The idea that I was going to get on a touring bus and travel all day and night to San Antonio seemed ludicrous. Any constant motion like a moving bus would certainly set it off again, I thought. And then there was the possibility that I'd have such an unnerving attack while in the middle of a song onstage in front of twenty thousand people. I could just see me falling off that stage in a state of complete delirium and panic.

I ended up missing the Country Radio Broadcasters ceremony—Teddy, Jeff, and Mark took the stage without me—and we had to cancel the San Antonio show. Reba McEntire stepped in at the last minute to replace us. Doctors immediately began to experiment on me, for lack of a better term, to find out what exactly was going on. They knew right away that it was much more than a "dizzy spell" brought on by twisting my neck too quickly. In the same way that chronic depression is not to be confused with occasionally feeling blue, chronic vertigo is far more complicated, and dangerous, than occasionally feeling dizzy. It's not something that you can just "snap out of."

Vertigo, they explained, as opposed to lightheadedness or dizziness, can be caused by a number of underlying disorders. There is something called benign paroxysmal positional vertigo (BPPV), a common form initiated by head movements. Maybe that's what I had. Dale felt that his vertigo was aggravated by the loud reverberations of a stadium full of screaming fans. Maybe twenty years of ear-piercing music and crowd noise had finally caught up with me. Or, more seriously, there's something called Ménièere's syndrome, which can cause abrupt, severe vertigo along with ringing in the ears and temporary hearing loss. My first episode, and subsequent ones, were certainly abrupt and severe. Or, even worse, vertigo can be a symptom of something catastrophic like multiple sclerosis. It can bring about vomiting, difficulty with speaking, and severe headaches.

In my case, they could never pin down just one explanation. We went from one doctor to another and test after test and never came home with a definitive answer. The thing that bothered me the most was that at least a couple of these doctors seemed to be more interested in experimenting with different drugs and therapies than in treating my problem. No matter what they did, the episodes kept occurring and in fact still come back, even today.

Vertigo can also be triggered by stress, and, Lord knows, it can cause stress. It makes you leery of doing anything or being in any situation where a sudden attack would render you incapacitated. Obviously, performing was my first concern, but also simple things like driving, flying, or anything else that might set off vibrations that could cause a sudden lack of equilibrium. I didn't drive for a long time after the initial incident for fear that I could be stricken on the road and end up being killed or killing someone else.

Oh, yeah, we were in the middle of a major tour at the time, the last major tour. If I had obeyed my initial impulse, before the idea of a farewell tour ever came up, to just get away for a year and not do anything musically except maybe write a song or two, a health problem like this would have been no big deal. But that option was long gone. We had major obligations—a whole year of shows—and I just couldn't *not* go onstage and do the job, vertigo or no vertigo.

After all those tests, we finally hit upon a regimen that allowed me to perform without the fear of falling being uppermost on my mind, not that it wasn't in the back of my mind at every concert. It was always a distraction to me and often a confidence deflator. I kept thinking of all the other sensations that might set it off—flashing cameras in the audience, for instance, or a wave of arm movements, or just the sheer reverberation from all the noise. In the end I got through it fine without any-one outside of our small circle of comrades even knowing there was a potential problem. I never fell or got nauseated or went into a strange state of altered consciousness. I did get sporadi-cally dizzy onstage, especially at my first performance after the initial attack, in Tallahassee, Florida. If I started feeling weird, I would simply grab the mike stand and hold on and hope to God the spell would pass before it got worse. It always did. I still had spells of vertigo, but thankfully, they didn't happen onstage to the point of causing a major disruption.

Kelly's reaction to all of this was blunt: "Frankly, I don't see how the guy did it. When vertigo hits me, I have to immediately withdraw, take some medication to calm me down and help me to sleep, and hope it's gone by the time I wake up. It was gut wrenching for me to see him up there. I mean, whether you're singing onstage or trying to do housework or office work, vertigo is vertigo. It doesn't matter. It has no mercy on anyone." It turns out she wasn't the only one with experience with vertigo—both Dale and Greg Fowler had been hit with it in the past. Dale summed up his view of my problem by saying, "Anyone any less dedicated would have announced he was going to take the next five years off and then walked away."

Unfortunately, much like the health scare I had in the early '90s, not everyone involved with Alabama was as understand-ing or forgiving. No doubt the stress of performing added to the stress of anticipating the vertigo, and I wasn't great at hiding this stress, but the cavalier attitude of some others was just plain hurtful. While I saw the situation as brutal and unforgiving—at the time, I considered it one of the most devastating things that had ever happened to me—others saw it as an overreaction to the pressures of the Farewell Tour or maybe another way for me to withdraw and feel sorry for myself.

I was taking medication that keyed me down and probably, to some, gave the appearance that I was distant and uninvolved. In this day and age, all it takes is for one surly or condescending comment to get out on the Internet before a world of bloggers thinks you're dogging it or playing for sympathy. I was doing neither. I was just trying to get through the show, give the audience their money's worth, and not blow it.

Long after the tour was over, I'm still trying to get a diagnosis that will help me combat this ailment. My symptoms now are intermittent motion movement, the sense that things around me are undulating and unstable and I can't quite get my bearings. I will continue to see doctors until we get it figured out. And maybe by writing about it here, people who are unfamiliar with vertigo's devastating effects or dismiss it in the same way we used to dismiss serious ailments like dyslexia or ADD will see it in a new and more understanding light.

The second round of farewell concerts was equally full of lasting memories, which I will attempt to capsulize by describing one event in Little Rock, Arkansas, on July 26, 2004. First, a little background: some time before that night, a young lady named Jennifer Leidel had shown up at a fan-appreciation event wearing a West Point cap, where she was attending at the time. The next thing I knew, we got a letter from First Lieutenant Jennifer Leidel, now with the 82nd Airborne Division in Iraq as a helicopter pilot. She said it was pretty rough over there and sent a picture in which she is holding an American flag up in front of her helicopter.

She and Kelly kept writing back and forth, and in her last correspondence she said she'd been told that she was coming home soon. Meanwhile, we heard that her best friend in Iraq had been shot down and killed while evacuating wounded soldiers. Very concerned, we tried to locate Jennifer. Finally Greg Fowler made a call to Fort Bragg, and there she was, back in the States and back in training for a new assignment.

We had hoped to meet up with Jennifer at a concert in Fayetteville, North Carolina, but for some reason she couldn't make it. Finally we arranged for her to come join us at the concert that night in Little Rock. We introduced her and her husband-to-be, Jason, onstage, and in a very touching gesture, she presented me with the very same flag she had proudly displayed in the photo from Iraq. It had served on many combat missions in the Iraq War. The audience reaction was overwhelming. I wouldn't trade that old flag for all the Grammys on earth.

At the same concert, Mike Huckabee, Arkansas governor at that time and later a candidate for president, came onstage to give us an award called the Arkansas Traveler Award, which is kind of like the key to the whole state. We'd already spent the day with the governor as he served up a great Southern meal at the newly refurbished governor's mansion that afternoon. To cap it all off, knowing that he was a pretty mean bass guitar player, we handed him Teddy's bass, and he played along with us to our song "I'm in a Hurry." We thought of asking him to join us on tour, but he already had a day job.

After Jennifer joined us in Little Rock, she asked if I would come down and sing the first song at her wedding reception in Sebring, Florida, that November. How could I turn down such an American hero? Soon after her wedding, unfortunately, Jennifer's life met with a cruel tragedy. She had survived the dangers of the war, but her husband, Jason, couldn't survive the dangers of driving on I-95 near Fayetteville, North Carolina. A truck came across the highway and hit their car head on. Jason was killed in the crash, and Jennifer suffered serious injuries but recovered. She has since remarried, and at the time of this writing, she is training other soldiers to fly helicopters at a base in Alabama.

At every stop on this last trip around the block, we wanted to thank not just soldiers like Jennifer who are out there working for the rest of us every day, but also all the people, from Dick Clark to all the stars who came whenever I called about Country Cares and the June Jam, to every last fan who made the whole damn thing possible in the first place. That's why I especially liked to sing "The Fans" night after night. "The Fans" was written by me, Teddy, and Greg, and is included in the very first *Alabama*

*Greatest Hits* CD in 1986. But it wasn't a hit, technically. It was never released as a single, so it never made an appearance on the country singles charts. We included it in that CD because it was an important message to our fans, and that was doubly so when we performed it for perhaps the last time onstage during the Farewell Tour.

As for all the others who have helped us along the way, that's an added blessing for sure. Marc Oswald, who had to ask a lot of people in the music business for favors surrounding the last tour, says people respond because Alabama's "kindness meter is off the charts." I'm not sure about that, but I do believe that when you extend kindness to others, no matter what the context, you inevitably get it back in spades. It is a guiding principle of Christian belief—it is better to give than receive—and much more spiritually enriching. Especially in an ego-driven business like country music, where most people most of the time are trying to claw their way up the ladder of success, it's gratifying to know that a lot of people—from Toby Keith or Kenny Chesney to the local radio programmers in Seattle or Tampa—are ready to jump at the chance to help out in an ever-widening circle of giving.

Finally, on October 16, 2004, we reached the farewell show of the farewell leg of the Farewell Tour, the end of the end of decades of touring. It was at the Civic Center in Bismarck, North Dakota, and though it wasn't snowing outside, it was cold. Damn near everyone involved in the history of Alabama who could still walk was there—Dale, Barbara, Greg, crew, staff, and most important for me, my whole immediate family. In an unreleased documentary of the Farewell Tour shot by Breck Larson, Mark says, "I think I'm in complete denial about all of this"—we all were—and you can see Kelly wipe a tear from her eye as I give her and the kids one big hug before I walk on that stage the last time.

To me, the whole concert was a blur. Marc Oswald remembers it being just as good as the first concert on the extended tour two years before. According to Randa, still just a teenager, the whole family stood offstage and cried the whole show. She goes on: "It was just so big for Dad and so big for all of us. Dad onstage had been my whole way of life my whole life! I remember they played the song 'The Fans' and really from the heart, and we just couldn't believe it. An era of our life was over. It was all really weird for me, because you don't know what God has planned next, so it was a great feeling to know that we would have him home but weird because all of this was going to be over. I mean . . . boy . . ."

It was hard not to pause at the end of every song in the set to realize that I wouldn't be singing that one again with Alabama for who knows how long. At the end of the last song of the evening, "Mountain Music," we decided it was time to bring everyone in our little family onstage so they could all take a bow. We got them all up there—Dale, Barbara, Greg, big Steve Boland, my one-man security force of years and years, all the sound engineers, lighting guys, roadies, and bus and truck drivers. Each and every one of them came to the microphone at center stage, said who they were, where they were from, and what they did. It took about thirty minutes, but no one left the hall. The fans understood that as a working family, we were saying good-bye to one another at the same time we were saying good-bye to them. I must admit, I got a little emotional up there. Many of these people had been watching Alabama's back for literally decades. This wasn't, "See you at the next gig." This was, "Hey, it's over."

Greg Fowler was nice enough to jot down my final words onstage that night. It wasn't a flowery farewell speech, but it came directly from my heart: "My name is Randy Owen," I said. "I play guitar and sing for the group Alabama. And I love you, and I always will. God bless ya'll very much."

Afterward, back in the dressing room, we threw an impromptu party and sat around and cried and high-fived one another and told lies and drank champagne. Toasts were made, and again it was very emotional. It was just a great feeling to be there together and look back in wonder at what we all had accomplished as a single unit. It was long past the point for personal differences and petty complaints. All long-lasting musical groups change; people leave out of "creative differences," or someone dies prematurely from drugs or alcohol, or—like with the Beatles—the whole thing blows apart at once. In that dressing room that night stood the same three guys who started the thing in their teens and early twenties and a drummer who had joined up about the point we went from small time to big. Four guys, twenty-five years of continual success—that was definitely something to drink to.

And then we all got on the bus and went home.

Home for most of us was the same place—Fort Payne. After every tour we went home—the married guys went home to their families, the bachelors and bachelorettes went home to their one-two-or-three-roommate houses, often right across the street from one another. No one flew off to California or Miami. We'd bump into one another pumping gas or buying groceries. Then the call would come, and we'd gather and hit the road again. We lived on pretty much the same schedule, year after year after year.

And then, all of a sudden, we didn't. We still saw each other down at the Strand or buying a birthday present at Martin's Jewelry on Gault Avenue. It wasn't like the members of an army unit that went back to the base, turned in their gear, and then dispersed back to their hometowns. It was a little surreal. Everything was the same but radically different at the same time. It wasn't like we had been drummed out of the business and had to hide out in Fort Payne. We just came to a point and stopped.

On the unreleased documentary, Dale pretty much said it all: "We all know that everything has to come to an end. Everything.

"But there will never be another Alabama."

# CHAPTER 11

# MAY THE CIRCLE
# BE UNBROKEN

*There's a place where I live called the Canyon*
*Where Daddy taught me to swim*
*And that water, it's so pure*
*And I'm gonna make sure*
*Daddy's grandkids can swim there like him*

"PASS IT ON DOWN" BY TEDDY GENTRY, RANDY OWEN,
RONNIE ROGERS, AND WILL ROBINSON

So I went back to doing what I needed to get good at—getting up every morning and slowing down. For the first time in decades, I didn't have to look at a booking sheet or an interview schedule before I could decide what to do that day. I could breathe deep, take care of my health, be with family and friends, and de-stress.

I was back to seeing my mama and sisters often, and being around Mama on a more regular basis is a surefire way of coming back down to reality. For all those years, through all the Alabama triumphs, accolades, and constant media attention, she pretty much stuck to her guns and lived the same life she was living the day I took off for the wilds of Myrtle Beach. She worked at the sock mill until her back gave out, played the piano in public every chance she got, and rarely left her mountain home. As Randa once said, "She's a feisty, feisty woman," sure in her ways and not given to airs of any kind.

I long ago gave up trying to "improve" her life in any way with the conveniences of modern living. If I ask her if there is anything I could buy her that might please her, her reply is "No. Most of that stuff don't bother me one bit 'cause I don't want it, I've got enough, the Lord's blessed me with enough."

When was the last time you heard anyone in this consumer-crazy country say they have "enough"? What about a new TV? "I don't need another TV, as long as this one's playing, which it is, thank you."

If she wants butter, she gets out her electric churning machine. If she wants biscuits or bread, she makes them. If she wants vegetables, she goes out to her garden and picks them. What about going out to dinner? "I'd rather fix my own food and eat at home as to go out and pay people a big price for something I could make myself. That's true. I mean that from my heart."

She just feels like the world doesn't owe her anything. One night Alison and I were at home when Mama called and said, "Son, you at home? I need you to come over here." I immediately knew something was wrong. I thought maybe someone had broken in and accosted her. Alison and I rushed over, gun in hand, ready to kick some butt. We found Mama lying in bed, no intruder in sight.

She had fallen, she explained, her leg was bleeding, and her arm was extended straight out and slightly twisted. She said, "Listen, son, can you put this arm back right? Just turn it back around, it'll be fine."

I said, "Mama, your arm is broken."

She said, "Oh, it'll be okay as soon as you put it back right."

We put a coat over her nightgown, took her down to the hospital, and got her arm set and bandaged up. She went along with it all but never understood what all the fuss was about. I just wonder how many times when she was growing up that someone just jerked on a broken bone, put it back in place, and let the bone just heal itself? That's why I drive by her house every morning and honk. At seventy-six, she shouldn't be setting her own bones.

If the old mantra was "The music comes first," then the new one in the time immediately following the Farewell Tour was probably "The land and the cattle come first." By that time our two oldest kids were pretty much out on their own, and Randa, in high school, loved tending the land and raising cattle as much as Kelly and I did. Over the years we've acquired our land piece by piece, buying most of it from people who probably bought it from people I knew growing up. I still refer to certain parcels as the King place, or the Holbrook place, or the Copeland place, or the Jackson place, even though the former owner of that last place, Clyde Jackson, the man who sold my mama and daddy their second forty acres, is long gone.

To me, every parcel has a story. I look at one piece and say to myself, *I used to plow a mule there with Mr. Copeland.* Or that land down by the creek, I swapped for some land I owned down in south Alabama because timber companies don't like to operate up here on this mountain because of the freezing rain and sleet. And then I bought the King place and then several acres from the original Crow place, then the Holbrook place . . . you get the idea.

Naming those names and remembering the lives behind them is part of a whole sense of belonging. There's nothing that I can think of that would bother me more than being in a place where I didn't know anybody. Some people can live in big, anonymous cities and have a network of a few scattered friends. I guess I'm not one of them.

We have about two thousand acres now, most of it contiguous, most of it connected to the past, and none of it getting prepared for new housing developments. Being the caretaker of all that land can be a big job. Many people have the misconception that if you just leave land to grow wild, it's good for the local wildlife. That's not true. Quail, for instance, flourish in an environment of small farms and especially those growing cotton and corn. The little chicks love to run out into the fields, eat the insects for protein, then scurry back to cover. If they have to run through a lot of tall, uncultivated grass to get to that food, their wings will get wet from the grass dew, and they'll die before they get back to their mother. The same with baby turkeys. Mother turkeys are notoriously bad mothers and will drag their poults through wet grass in search of grasshoppers. Many of them won't survive. If you have some mowed strips where they can move around easily, they'll thrive.

On the other hand, they all need woods for protection, so we have to maintain the woodland in a way that deer, for instance, can gobble down some of the wild broom sage in the fields, then hide out in the woods when they hear my truck coming down the road. I love to watch how the pine forests around here, no matter how much you cut them back, just come back thicker than before, with trees providing cover and nutrition for animals big and small.

When the weather's right, I'm outdoors, trimming trees, mowing grass, or maybe casting a line on one of our fourteen lakes. But my main activity, perhaps the most relaxing one for me, is looking at cows and calves. To get around, I usually take one of Daddy's favorite old trucks I still cherish—the '68 Ford Ranger or a '71 dual-wheeled Chevy with a cattle bed. As I mentioned, we now have almost a thousand head of cattle, most of them registered, polled Herefords or Angus. And a lot of them are calves, maybe 170 to 200 at any one time. We watch them grow up and try to make sure they are healthy and disease free, and then many of them join other cattle for one of our two annual sales—the official Tennessee River Music Dixieland Delight Hereford Sale, on the Saturday before Memorial Day, and the official Tennessee River Music Dixieland Delight Angus Sale, on the first Saturday after Thanksgiving.

As I'm writing this, we have just celebrated our twenty-fifth consecutive year of holding the Hereford sale out at the ranch, and by the time you're reading this, we'll have staged our seventh annual Angus sale. The Hereford auction was a big event, as usual, both a business gathering and simply a gathering of like-minded people, farm families and their kids and grandma and all the rest. Before it's all said and done, there could be fifteen hundred people coming up here to talk highly bred cattle, inspect them, trade breeding tips, and even buy a few.

They start showing up on Friday, our sales catalog in hand, to look at all the cattle we put on display before the actual sale. They walk around and take notes, and then we feed them some good old Southern cooking. They're back on Saturday for the actual sale, which is run much like any kind of auction. The cattle are brought into a ring, lot by lot, and an auctioneer runs the bidding while ring men filter through the crowd and spot the bidders. One lot may have two or three animals in it. When we're all done, we've sold around 75 to 100 registered cattle. Then we feed the crowd again and they head home.

The annual Dixieland Delight sale is an important part of our cattle operation, but it's also another excuse to invite a large crowd up to the ranch and wade into the community of people we feel so much a part of. We also have an annual Fan Appreciation Day every June where fans show up, and I thank them by putting out a big spread and singing a few of their favorites songs. Then, as I mentioned before, there is our annual golf tournament every April to help out Alabama Sheriff's Youth

Ranches. I don't have it at the ranch—it's usually held at a different Alabama golf course—but it has the same homegrown spirit. We've been doing this for twenty-one years now and will continue until I can no longer swing a golf club. This last year we had, among others, two Baseball Hall of Fame players, Johnny Bench and Gaylord Perry, "Nashville Star" winner Angela Hacker, two other rising Nashville stars, David St. Romain and James LeBlanc, and perhaps country music's most unique celebrity, Big & Rich's pal, Two Foot Fred.

Even when the Tennessee River Music ranch isn't full of people, it's still a zoo. We have three horses that technically belong to Randa, but we take care of them while she's in college, plus two dogs, a yard full of chickens, a menagerie of cats, a flock of Canadian geese, and all of those ponds full of fish. And, oh yeah, a thousand or so cows. Kelly had a tribe of goats for a while but had to let them go because she didn't have time to properly tend to them.

We also make it our mission to rescue stray dogs we find on the highway. Kelly or I will pick them up and bring them home, get them checked out by a vet and neutered or spayed, then put them up for adoption. Right now we have six rescue dogs boarding with us, waiting for new homes.

So the ranch makes for a lot of work and returns a lifetime full of pleasure and satisfaction. Physically and mentally, I needed a long break from both Alabama and the music business in general, and the ranch was an idyllic retreat. There was no break in my ongoing obligations to St. Jude, Country Cares, the scholarship program for young Alabama farmers, my board position at Jacksonville State University, and other like ventures. But in all of these areas, I was no longer beholden to the collective pressures and responsibilities of that musical institution called Alabama. I was now solely in charge of my own life.

I think it was inevitable that after a long resting period, I would get back to music in some way. It had been in my blood since my daddy handed me that first Stella guitar. I had never really stopped writing songs. If a song idea came to me while out working on the ranch, I would come home and fool around with a new lyric or melody. In the middle of the final tour, for instance, my beloved Paw Paw died at age ninety-three, but only later did I have a chance to commemorate his life in a song. The song is called "Good," and in part it says:

> For 73 years he raised seven children
> With the help of Mama's mom
> But on the day he was buried
> There at Mount Zion
> I thought he's in a real good place

I never thought I was totally dried up or ready to "retire," whatever that means these days. I also felt then, and continue to feel, that Alabama's days are far from over. Since the Farewell Tour, I have produced two inspirational albums, and I'm sure there's a lot more work in us as a group. After my hiatus, though, I felt I still needed to spread my own wings a little. I needed my own new direction.

Like most things in my life, that new direction—my first solo album—came about organically. I came to realize that in order to be an active presence and force in the work I was doing with St. Jude and others, I had to stay current. There was some research done at St. Jude that indicated that a lot of people they were trying to reach had never heard of Danny Thomas. At first I found that shocking, until I thought about it for a minute. A seventeen-year-old today wasn't even born before Danny passed away and would only know about *Make Room for Daddy* if he or she sat in front of the cable network TV Land all day.

For Country Cares alone, I had to stay current with country radio in order to ensure the continued enthusiastic participation of hundreds of country DJs. Audiences are forever changing. Every year country music draws in new, younger listeners. A new audience demands new music, and I felt it was time to deliver some.

It's like that old Paul McCartney joke. "Who is he?" one teenager asks another. "Oh, you remember—he was once a part of that group Wings." The Beatles, to them, was ancient history.

By the time I released the first single—"Braid My Hair"—off of my first solo album, it had been almost eight years since I had sung a brand-new song for country radio. Plus, I had never performed onstage as a solo act—never. I was pretty sure I could pull it off, but I wouldn't know until I tried it. New act, new music, maybe even a new haircut—sounded like the right thing to do.

I talked to Kelly about it, and she was definitely on board. Dale Morris had the brilliant idea of matching me with John Rich as a producer. Besides being the nattily dressed half of one of the hottest groups in country music, Big & Rich, John is probably the most prolific songwriter-producer in Nashville at this writing. And after sitting down with him, I realized he was a lot like me. He had a fierce determination to be successful and was willing to try damn near anything to make something new and fresh. With Big & Rich, it was the idea of adding new lyrics. With Gretchen Wilson and "Redneck Woman," it was the raw, unadorned energy of one tough, no-BS woman. With Randy Owen, it turned out, it was the very personal approach of the album we created together, *One on One*.

After John and I sat down and wrote a couple of songs together, I still had to be convinced that this solo thing was the right move. I mean, what if I went out there to perform and people didn't really want to see me sing by myself? So with the help of Dale, Barbara, Marc Oswald, and Shawn Pennington, we put together a crack new band and went out and did a dozen or so concerts in a variety of venues, from Lake Geneva, Wisconsin to the Alabama Theatre in Myrtle Beach. When I got back home, I was totally convinced that this was what I needed to do.

In order for the album to be all that I wanted it to be, I felt like I needed a song that might really stand out as an anthem of sorts for all the kids I'd tried to help over the years and all the ones who still needed our help. Then I remembered a song that had miraculously come my way a few months before.

The song was called "Braid My Hair."

The two men who wrote "Braid My Hair"—Chris Gray and Brent Wilson—were frustrated when they first tried to get me to listen to their song. At the time, I was taking my long holiday from the musical life, and recording anything was the furthest thing from my mind. So, hitting a brick wall with me, they did an end around and sent it to my mama. They were not the first people to do this, but my mama rarely listens to the songs that are sent to her, and the ones she does listen to, she never likes. Usually sending a song to her is a waste of postage. I wouldn't recommend it.

Well, this song she listened to and liked. As Chris later said, "If you want to get a song published, go to the best song plugger in the business—Martha Owen!" Mama gave me the CD and said, "You know, you might want to listen to this one." I was shocked to hear her say that—she had never recommended a song, period—so I said, "Tell me more."

"It's about a little girl," she said, "who is losing her hair because of cancer, and she wants to grow it back. It's real sweet."

It was more than sweet. It was awesome. Here are the opening lyrics:

> She could be the first female president
> Or be the doctor whose experiment
> Finds the cure to what she's in here for
> But right now treatments keep her sick in bed
> That baseball cap never leaves her head

I loved the song and had never heard anything quite like it. It grew out of Chris's experience working as a teacher in a children's hospital, helping young patients keep up with their schoolwork while undergoing chemotherapy and other treatments for cancer and other serious ailments. He knew all about hair loss during chemo and knew that every young girl who suffered through that experience dreamed of again having hair to braid. As soon as he mentioned that to Brent, they had the hook—"braid my hair"— for a great song.

> *I wanna go to school, make a friend, be able to run again*
> *Take off my mask and just breathe in the air*
> *But most of all, I'm gonna braid my hair*

I reached Chris and Brent in Nashville and found out that they had never had a song recorded before. They said they obviously wanted me to do the song after following my activities with Country Cares and St. Jude. I told them I didn't have anything going at the time, but that I would be in touch if I did.

After I decided to make a solo album, I knew this song was a perfect fit, so I called them immediately, and, thank God, no one had yet recorded it. At that point we decided the song was so close to the everyday reality of the kids at St. Jude—many of whom are undergoing chemo and losing their hair—that it was only natural that St. Jude profit from its release. It would fit nicely into the latest annual Country Cares campaign, a way, really, of invigorating the whole effort. We decided to premiere it at the same time we launched Country Cares again, and we ended up working a deal where the hospital will receive 100 percent of all publishing royalties earned by the song, as well as have a piece of the action of every digital MP3 download of the song. Handing over the publishing was a generous gesture on the part of Chris and Brent, but their hearts were definitely in the right place or they wouldn't have come up with such a moving song in the first place. I can only hope this propels them into superstardom as a songwriting team.

In the midst of all of this—finishing the new CD, *One on One*, releasing the single of "Braid My Hair," and easing back into performing—I got a call from John Moses at St. Jude with another incredible blessing. As a former recipient, John was allowed to nominate his own candidates for a very prestigious award called the Ellis Island Medal of Honor. The award is given annually by the National Ethnic Coalition to American citizens they deem to have made significant contributions to the United States while maintaining their ethnic or ancestral identity. Unbeknownst to me, John submitted my name as a candidate, and I was chosen.

The awards ceremony was held on Ellis Island in the Port of New York, and the list of recipients on hand was mind-boggling. Among the 106 honorees were seven prominent Indian Americans in fields from broadcasting to medicine; former U.S. senator and Native American Ben Nighthorse Campbell; actor Gary Sinise, Lieutenant Dan from *Forrest Gump*, active in working with disabled war veterans and the founder of Operation Iraqi Children, a group sending school supplies to Iraqi kids; General Duncan McNabb, Vice Chief of Staff for the U.S. Air Force; and Rwanda-born Jacqueline Murekatete, who saw her whole family slaughtered in the 1994 genocide there and now works to end genocide everywhere. Every age, race, ethnicity, religion, and culture was represented there—all of them Americans, all of them dedicated to improving the lives of others—and I felt so humbled to be in their presence. I felt like I wasn't there just representing myself and my family but also my ethnic and cultural origins—from the rural farm life of DeKalb County to the state of Alabama and the region of the American South that I love so much.

And so, a trip to Ellis Island and a new solo venture aside, I'd guess you'd have to say that I'm back to pretty much where I started. I live where my parents lived and their parents lived, and I live with the constant daily reminder of the exact places where my daddy and I would pick cotton all day or the exact road we would take to First Monday in Scottsboro or the exact woods where we would walk and he'd point out the difference between a post oak and a white oak. I don't live in the past, that's for sure, but I certainly live *with* the past. And that's the way I've always wanted it.

There's still a lot for me to do in this life. With the *One on One* CD out there, there's still a lot more music to make, more money to raise for St. Jude, and a hundred other worthy causes, and even a few more cattle to breed and sell on auction day. Not too long ago someone asked me why, after all those years with Alabama, I was out writing and performing music again. I thought for a minute, then answered, "Well, I want to keep making new music and keep going until I'm old enough to play the halftime show at the Super Bowl."

There's always a new dream around every corner. I plan to keep on playing as long as people keep on listening.

On top of it all, there is life with Kelly and our wonderful kids and hopefully, before too long, some grandkids. Pretty soon I'll be the Paw Paw in the family. I'll be the old guy telling stories of singing schools and my daddy and Buck Owens harmonizing on "Love's Gonna Live Here Again" at six in the morning and the time I cut my thumb off or got stuck under the house trying to gather some chicken eggs. And when I start to forget some of the details—or someone asks me if "chert rock" is a real word—I'll have this book to look things up.

I'm sure one day one of those grandkids will ask me, in so many words, "Why you, Paw Paw? Why, among the thousands and thousands of guitar-loving rural kids in the American South, were you and Teddy and Jeff so extremely fortunate? Why were you given a path out of poverty and handed such a rich and plentiful life?"

And I'll say something like, "Because that was God's plan for me. He's had His hand on me the whole time. And you know what? He's got a plan for you too. And I can't wait to see what it is."

## ACKNOWLEDGMENTS

*Thanks to:* God, who's "brought me safe thus far."

*My late father:* the friend I miss daily. I can't overemphasize his impact on my life. Thanks "G.Y."

*My mother, Martha:* who, along with Daddy, "G.Y.," got the most out of the least of finances. Thanks to them for the true love I saw shared by two incredible Christian parents who walked the walk and talked the talk.

*My grandparents:* who raised large families (twelve and seven, respectively) and farmed the soil, living a faithful, married life till their deaths. Especially Paw Paw Teague for the "I'm proud of you son" conversations.

*My sisters:* Reba and Rachel, who shared the love of our parents.

*The military men and women:* who have served, are serving, and will serve our great country.

*Dale and Earline Morris:* who are part of my heart and family.

*My buddies at Dale Morris & Assoc.:* Barbara, Sue, and Jamie.

*The "Ro" team:* Marc Oswald, Shawn Pennington, Sheila Hozhabri, Will Hitchcock, Steve Boland, Craig Campbell, Jennie Smythe, and all the folks at Broken Bow Records.

*The road crew:* Jim Henson, Paul Scodova, William "Eto" Farley, Jere "Hollywood" Galloway, and Will Stinson.

*The Great Band:* Megan Mullins, John Bohlinger, Chuck Tilley, Kim Fleming, Aaron Mason, David Ridley, John Howard, Wade Hayes, Steve Mandile, and Steve Peffer.

*To everyone in country radio:* for playing the music and for Country Cares.

*A big thanks to Allen Rucker:* for his help assembling my ramblings on this book.

*The guys in Alabama* and the magic we created.

*Everyone at the Bowery in Myrtle Beach, S.C.:* who are a part of my history.

*All the road crews, stage crews, drivers, record label staffs and techs:* whoever worked for Alabama.

*Ralph Seagraves and T. Wayne Robinson at RJ Reynolds:* who took the music to places impossible to go without them

*Chief Jordan and Billy Bullock:* who told me to "stick to it."

*Tommy Arrington:* who gave us our only bonus.

*The lady who fired us at the Thunderbird Motel.*

*Sonny and Linda Reece:* whose encouragement was pivotal.

*All the friends who worked all over the Grand Strand:* who encouraged me to write and sing.

*Greg Fowler:* unofficial member of the band and co-writer of songs.

*All the great promotion teams at RCA:* I know I wouldn't be here without them.

*All the writers of all the great songs I've gotten to sing.*

*Kelly's mom, June, and dad, Jim, and her family:* and for June's Lemon Blueberry Bread. I've tried really hard to take good care of their little girl and their three beautiful grandchildren, Alison, Heath, and Randa.

*Harold Shedd, the quiet genius, and all the studio guys—Jim Cotton, George Clinton, and Joe Scaife—and the pickers who grooved to a bunch of hits.*

*All the producers:* Rick Hall, James Stroud, Barry Beckett, Josh Leo, Emory Gordy Jr., and Garth Fundis.

*The fans:* I don't have enough thank-you's to say—just know that nobody could ever appreciate more the support you have given me.

*The book people:* Roger Freet, Mel Berger, Allen Rucker, and Suzanne Wickham.

*My buddies who were classmates* at Adamsburg Junior High, Fort Payne High School, Northeast Alabama Community College, and Jacksonville State University.

*My brothers at Pi Kappa Phi:* our lives have touched and I'm better for it.

*My mother:* who was my preschool teacher and all the incredible teachers and professors I've had.

*The president at Jacksonville State University:* who gave me permission to graduate absentee, to go to Myrtle Beach to join up again with whom was to become Alabama.

*Waylon Jennings:* for the talks after the shows.

*Johnny and June Cash:* for that day at the restaurant in Paso Robles.

*Conway Twitty:* for the phone call about "Lady Down On Love."

*Loretta Lynn:* for the lipstick messages.

*Tammy Wynette:* for being so real.

*Dolly Parton:* for the June Jam, and for "Holding Everything."

*Willie Nelson:* for the June Jam.

*Hank Williams Jr.:* For recording "Tennessee River."

*Ralph Stanley:* for "Thomas."

*Roger Miller and Mel Tillis:* for the funny stories in the studio.

*Garth Brooks:* for the June Jam.

*Reba McEntire:* for the "Presentation."

*Alan Jackson and Neal McCoy:* for playing the most June Jams.

*Barbara Mandrell:* for the TV show.

*Jo Walker Meador:* for the CMA.

*Bob Romeo and the ACM.*

*Bob Johnson:* Channel 9

*Jerry Hayes:* Channel 19

*Merle Haggard:* for the stories after the shows and for "Sing Me Back Home."

*Chet Atkins:* for liking my vocal.

*Del Bryant and Everyone at BMI.*

*Buck Borders:* for taking care of my family financially.

*Everyone who helped at the Fan Club.*

*Bill Scruggs, Mike Milom, Keith Fowler, and George Moffett.*

*All the volunteers at all of the June Jams and to everyone I left out unintentionally.*

*Eddy Arnold:* for offering to help financially.

*Frances Preston:* for the writer's advance—BMI.

*Charley and Rozene Pride:* still close friends and for the encouragement on "Tennessee River."

*Moe Bandy:* for the kind words on "My Home's in Alabama."

*Jerry Bradley, Joe Galante, Butch Waugh, Tony Brown, Sheila and Benny Shipley, and Cynthia:* RCA/BMG.

*Mariam Williams:* for the Hollywood Walk of Fame.

*Dick Clark, Bill Boyd, Gene Weed:* my dear friends in Los Angeles, CA, for their work with the American Music Awards and the ACM.

*The Southern Rockers:* who influenced my approach to the stage show—Lynyrd Skynyrd, Marshall Tucker Band, CDB, and the Allman Brothers Band.

*Rascal Flatts* for the Medallion Ceremony; *Sawyer Brown* for the Medallion Ceremony; *Kenny Chesney* for singing "Lady Down on Love" at the Medallion Ceremony—and for "My Home" in Birmingham's performance.

As the lead singer of the legendary group Alabama, Randy Owen would appear to have seen and done it all—73 million albums sold, countless miles on the road touring, a warehouse full of awards, and a coveted spot in the Country Music Hall of Fame. Yet this singer/songwriter/entertainer/rancher/family man is embarking on a new path—a solo career with a new album, *One On One*, set for a November 4, 2008, release; a national tour with a ten-piece band; and an attitude that rivals that of a brand-new artist.

"I'm as excited about this as I've ever been," said Randy. "Before I decided to do the solo thing, we put a band together and did some dates late last year to see if the fans were still out there. When I came back I was totally convinced we needed to do this."

Randy teamed up with John Rich to produce *One On One* for the powerhouse indy label Broken Bow Records. The multifaceted Rich, who has produced Gretchen Wilson, his own duo Big & Rich, James Otto, Jewel, and John Anderson's critically acclaimed *Easy Money* album, jumped at the chance to work with the legend. "John's so smart about what he wants to hear," said Randy of the experience. "And the musicians he works with in the studio understand what he wants. We really took our time with it and didn't rush it, and I'm really pleased with what we came out with."

His long connection with his fans is the exact reason he titled the album *One On One*. "I feel like this album is a real personal thing—me to you," he says passionately. "The song 'One On One' is one of the most personal songs on the album."

Randy wrote or co-wrote seven of the eleven cuts on the new album, and one of the songs, "Braid My Hair," came to him in a very creative manner. Writers Chris Gray and Brent Wilson—who never had a song released as a single—knew Randy Owen was the man to cut the song but ran into brick walls on every avenue they used to get the song to him. Chris finally tracked down the address of Randy's mother's house and sent the song to her. She listened to the song, liked it, and passed it along to her son.

"I said, 'Mama, I'm so sorry people send you these songs,' and she said, 'Well, you might want to listen to that one,'" recalled Randy. "So I listened to it four or five times, and I thought 'Wow, what a song.'"

The writers generously agreed to donate 100 percent of the publishing proceeds from the song to St. Jude Children's Research Hospital. "How much more loving and compassionate can you get than that song?" asked Randy. "It's so real, and I've seen this lived out over and over at St. Jude. It's an incredible story done in song. To kick this album off with this song is definitely the right way to go."

"Like I Never Broke Her Heart," written by Shannon Lawson, Mitzi Dawn, and J. T. Harding, is the album's first single released to radio. "When I first heard this I thought it was one of the greatest titles I'd ever heard," Randy admits. "This is one of those great songs I like to wrap myself around and really get into."

For over twenty-five years Randy has been the front man and lead vocalist of one of the most prolific groups in the history of music. The band signed a recording contract with RCA Records in 1980, launching a career that to date has resulted in twenty-one gold, platinum, and multiplatinum albums; forty-two number-one singles; and, again, over seventy-three million albums sold. Alabama received over 150 industry awards, including eight country music "Entertainer of the Year" honors, two Grammys, two People's Choice Awards, and their very own star on the Hollywood Walk of Fame. They were named Artist of the Decade by the Academy of Country Music in 1989 and Country Group of the Century by the Recording Industry Association of America in 1999. In November 2005, Randy and his Alabama band mates received country music's highest honor, being inducted into the Country Music Hall of Fame.

"I'm very proud of everything we accomplished, and I hold what we did with Alabama as a very sacred part of my life," Randy concludes.

Randy's passion for helping others is evident through the types of causes he and the band choose to support. Alabama played an integral role in raising millions of dollars for schools, public service organizations, hospitals, youth ranches, and scholarships. But no organization is dearer to Randy's heart than the St. Jude Children's Research Hospital.

In 1989, Randy was asked to address the Country Radio Seminar in Nashville following the death of Danny Thomas, who was to be the seminar's keynote speaker. Inspired by the dreams and determination of St. Jude Children's Research Hospital founder Danny Thomas, Randy offered a challenge to those in attendance to accept Danny's dream of eradicating childhood cancers and other catastrophic diseases. Randy delivered the message well, and country radio accepted the challenge with passion. "Country Cares for St. Jude Kids" was born.

"I called it the 'Miracle on Beale Street,'" said Randy, referring to St. Jude being based in Memphis and the city's most famous street.

The national radiothon program is today the most successful radio fundraiser in history. Hundreds of radio stations and the entire music industry have joined hands and forces to fight the never-ending battles of childhood cancer and other diseases. The events have raised an astounding $345 million since Randy's challenge in 1989.

For Randy's efforts, Tony Thomas, son of St. Jude founder Danny Thomas, presented him with the prestigious Founder's Award—an honor Danny only bestowed on very special occasions—last year. In accepting the award, Randy acknowledged the fans of country music, the men and women of country radio, and the country music industry for embracing Danny's dream.

In addition, Randy was honored to receive the Paul G. Rogers Award for Public Service and also received a prestigious Ellis Island Medal of Honor this year. In June, he accepted a National

Association of Broadcasters (NAB) Service to America Award
on behalf of St. Jude for their "Country Cares for St. Jude Kids"
radiothon program.

When not on the road promoting his music career, Randy
can be found operating his successful working cattle ranch,
named Tennessee River Music, on the grounds of his Lookout
Mountain boyhood family farm. Tennessee River Music has
garnered many national, regional, and state championships in
the registered Polled Hereford Breed. In May, Randy hosted his
twenty-fifth major cattle sale at his ranch. Each year he performs
at the event, and all concert proceeds are donated to the Hereford
Youth Foundation, which is dedicated exclusively to scholarship and educational support of youth in the business of raising
Hereford cattle.

No one would blame Randy Owen if he decided to sit back
and enjoy his legendary status as one of the founding members
and lead vocalist of the Recording Industry Association of America Country Group of the Century, yet his heart still burns to take
new music to the fans who have been touched by his words and
his music. *One On One*—both on radio and on stage—is sure to
give back to the fans what God has given him.

"I still love to get out and play. I'm head over heels into this
album, and I'm in it for the long run."

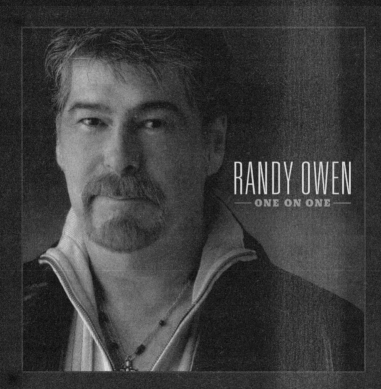